OLD AGE POPULATION IN INDIA

Issues, Programmes, Policies and Social Work Intervention

About the Editors

Prof. Subhabrata Dutta, Ph.D, M.Phil, PGCRM, MSW is Professor and Former Head, Department of Social Work and Former Dean of Students' Welfare, Assam University (A Central University), Silchar, India. He was an academic fellow at George Mason University in Washington DC, USA. So far fourteen scholars have completed Ph.D. under his guidance. He has published six books so far as author and coauthor. Prof. Dutta has completed five projects sponsored by Planning Commission, NITI AAYOG, Government of India, Ministry of Urban Affairs, Government of Assam and UNICEF Assam. He has contributed around 20 referred articles and 15 research papers in different Indian and International journals, edited and as editorial page pieces in leading Indian Newspapers (*The Statesman*). He is associated with several professional bodies like, ICSD, NAPSWI, ISPSW etc.

Dr. Ritwika Rajendra, Ph.D., MSW is an assistant Professor, Department of Social Work, Assam University, Silchar (A Central University), India. She has completed a project sponsored by NITI AAYOG, Government of India. She has presented more than 15 papers in National and International seminars. She has published papers in peer review journal, and also contributed chapters in edited books. She has conducted various field studies on the issue of women development through entrepreneurship. Dr. Rajendra acted as a field work co-ordinator in the department of Social Work, Assam University, Silchar. She is a member of NAPSWI.

OLD AGE POPULATION IN INDIA

Issues, Programmes, Policies and Social Work Intervention

Edited by

Subhabrata Dutta

Ritwika Rajendra

CONCEPT PUBLISHING COMPANY PVT. LTD.

NEW DELHI - 110 059

ISBN: 978-93-5594-151-0

First Published 2023

Published and Printed by

Concept Publishing Company Pvt. Ltd.
A/15-16, Commercial Block, Mohan Garden
New Delhi-110059 (India)
T : +91-11-41101460
E: publishing@conceptpub.com, W: www.conceptpub.com

Cataloging in Publication--Courtesy: D.K. Agencies (P) Ltd. <docinfo@dkagencies.com>

Old age population in India : issues, programmes, policies and social work intervention / edited by Subhabrata Dutta, Ritwika Rajendra.
pages cm
Contributed articles.
Includes bibliographical references and index.
ISBN 9789355941510

1. Older people--Government policy--India. 2. Older people--Health and hygiene--India. 3. Older people--Services for--India. I. Dutta, Subhabrata, 1973- editor. II. Rajendra, Ritwika, editor.

LCC HV1484.I4O43 2023 | DDC 362.60954 23

Foreword

With the development of medical science, the life span of human beings has increased. In this regard, I wish to mention that according to World Population Prospects 2019 (United Nations, 2019), by 2050, 1 in 6 people in the world will be over the age of 65, up from 1 in 11 in 2019. In the case of India, the population aged 65 years or over in 2030, will be more than around 13 crore against 8.7 crore in 2019, so more discussion on ageing is the sine qua non. It has to be mentioned that ageing is an irreparable biological process and is defined as the survival of the increasing number of individuals, who have completed their adult roles. Ageing is stated as the inevitable consequence of the decline in productiveness. With the advent of technology and modernization, there has been a decrease in the mortality rate, an increase in awareness, nutrition, and advancement in healthcare facilities and an increase in life expectancy. The aged people are experiencing changes in their social lives. In India, there has been an increase in the number of older persons. The aged people in India, experience various types of problems. These are social, economic, psychological, health, crime and violence, abuse and other miscellaneous problems. It's true that both the Central Government and various state governments have introduced various welfare measures and schemes for the care and benefit of the old age population in India.

This volume, titled, *Old Age Population in India: Issues, Programmes, Policies and Social Work Intervention* comprises 15 chapters focussing on all the demographic, social, economic, financial, and health of the aged population and also addressed the policy and existing welfare services. The chapters also cover the problems, care and NGOs' support and suggestions for modification and change of existing services.

This book is an important contribution to the literature on geriatric studies by offering unique perspectives. The chapters on research-based studies add strength as these are primary studies. Hope the volume will provide students, scholars, policymakers and field practitioners with the integration of on-going subjects.

I congratulate both the authors Dr. Subhabrata Dutta, Professor, and Dr. Ritwika Rajendra, Assistant Professor, of the Department of Social Work, Assam University, Silchar for lucidly editing the volume.

Dr. Shankar Chatterjee
Former Professor & Head (CPME),
NIRD & PR (Govt. of India),
Hyderabad, India

1. Life Time Achievement Award from EAST (Environmental Advisory for Sustainable Trust), Tamil Nadu in 2019.
2. Man of Excellence Award from the Indian Achievers' Forum (IAF) for 2021-22.

Preface

More people are living into old age in this world than at any time in the past. But old age is often considered as a problem. Many people are searching to find better ways of living at their good old age. There are various efforts and social movements found in striving to produce a more positive social attitude to old age and elderly people. Population ageing is seen as a major force transforming relationships at various levels—in the health and social care system, in the economy, and in society as a whole. As a result, the future of old age has become an important and complex issue in the contemporary world. Accordingly, the phenomenon of ageing population is becoming a major concern for the policy makers all over the world, for both developed and developing nations, during last three decades. But the problems arising out of it will have varied implications for underdeveloped, developing and developed countries. Ageing of population is affected due to downward trends in fertility and mortality, i.e., due to low birth rates coupled with long life expectancies. In India, the size of the elderly population, i.e., persons above the age of 60 years is constantly growing. It is observed that percentage of aged 60 or more is rapidly swelling and even the percentage of persons above age 80 is going up over the years. For a developing country like India, this may pose mounting pressures on various socio-economic fronts including pension outlays, health care expenditures, fiscal discipline, savings levels etc. Again this segment of population faces multiple medical and psychological problems. There is an emerging need to pay greater attention to ageing-related issues and to promote holistic policies and programmes for dealing with the ageing society. Keeping all these issues in mind of elderly population we are bringing this book under the titled, *Old Age Population in India: Issues, Programmes, Policies and Social Work Intervention* with 15 papers prepared by the faculty, scholars, students of social sciences and field practitioners and administrators. The papers cover the demography of aged population, policy issues, practical situations at the reality level, available welfare services for the aged, their day to day life, problems, care and NGOs' support and suggestion plans for the government.

The book is an attempt to use the best of current research-informed insights to enable us to look into the futures of old age over the next generation and illustrating a range of key issues arising out of ageing population. This book also demonstrates the complexities of many questions involved, but at the same time the rewards that come from analysing both the options for social ageing as well as future scenarios. Social gerontology is currently a challenging and exciting endeavour and the purpose of this book is to provide readers with grounding in the variety of current debates—theoretical and empirical as well as practitioner-based.

Subhabrata Dutta
Ritwika Rajendra

Contents

List of Contributors

Amit Das, Faculty (Community Medicine), Diphu Medical College, Government of Assam,
Email: mswamit.das@gmail.com

Angshu Lama (Mrs.), Ph.D. Scholar, Dept. of Psychiatric Nursing, LGB Regional Institute of Mental Health, Tezpur,
Email: angshu.lama@gmail.com

Apurba Saha (Dr.), Assist. Professor, Dept. of Social Work, Tezpur University, **Email:** apurbasahapsw@gmail.com

Azmal Hussain, M.Com. Student, Assam University, Silchar,
Email: ajmalhussain212@gmail.com

Barsha Kalita, Assist. Professor, NERIM, Guwahati, Department of Social Work, Assam University Silchar, **Email:** 1990barsha@gmail.com

Debotosh Sinha, Professor, Department of Social Work, Visva-Bharati, Sriniketan, **Email:** sinha.debotosh@gmail.com

Dipak Sarkar, PG Student, NERIE (NCERT), Umiam, Shillong, Meghalaya,
Email: surajitkh6@gmail.com

Jayanta Thakuria, PG Student, NERIE (NCERT), Umiam, Shillong,
Email: surajitkh6@gmail.com

Jyoti Sing, PG Student Department of Law, Assam University, Silchar,
Email: jollyjyoti121@gmail.com

Kaivalya T. Desai, Assist. Professor, Department of Social Work, Assam University, Silchar, **Email:** kaivalya.desai@gmail.com

Md Abdul Ahad Barbhuiya, M.Com Student, Assam University, Silchar,
Email: ahad.ktg@gmail.com

Meisuangdai Gonmei, PG Student, NERIE (NCERT), Umiam, Shillong
Email: surajitkh6@gmail.com

Nitul Das, PG Student, NERIE (NCERT), Umiam, Shillomg,
Email: surajitkh6@gmail.com

Pranita Ghalay, PhD Scholar, Department of Social Work, Assam University Silchar, **Email:** pranita.ghalay@gmail.com

Ritwika Rajendra, Assist. Professor, Department of Social work, Assam University, Silchar, **Email:** ritwika.rajendra@gmail.com

Sabina Begam Ahmed, Ph.D. Scholar, Dept. of Social Work, Assam University, Silchar, **Email:** sabina.msw.aus@gmail.com

Seema R Nambiar, PG Student, NERIE (NCERT) Umiam, Shillong, **Email:** surajitkh6@gmail.com

Srishti Dey, PG Student, Department of Law, Assam University, Silchar, **Email:** srishtide15@gmail.com

Subhabrata Dutta, Professor, Department of Social Work, Assam University, Silchar, **Email:** sduttasw@gmail.com

Sudipta Biswas, PhD Scholar, Department of Social Work, Visva-Bharati, Sriniketan, **Email:** sudiptab13@gmail.com

Sukumar Pal, Assist. Professor, Department of Social Work, Visva-Bharati, Sriniketan, **Email:** sukumarpal66@gmail.com

Suraj Sharma, PG Student, NERIE (NCERT), **Email:** surajitkh6@gmail.com

Surajit Kar, B.Ed. Student, NERIE (NCERT), Umiam, Shillong, **Email:** surajitkh6@gmail.com

Sushama Mukherjee, Visiting Faculty, Adult Education, Rabindra Bharati University, Kolkata and Ph.D. Scholar, Department of Social Work, Assam University, Silchar, **Email:** sushamamukherjee17@gmail.com

Viveni H. Yeptho, MSW Student, NEISSR, Nagaland, **Email:** aveniyeptho2544@gmail.com

Yhunsille Seb, MSW Student, NEISSR, Nagaland, **Email:** yhunsinle19@gmail.com

Introduction

The phenomenon of population ageing is becoming a major concern for the policy makers all over the world, both for developed and developing countries. India too is not immune from this demographic change. By 2020, India has around 12 million elderly persons with difficulty in accomplishing activities of daily living. There will also be a surge of chronic illness, the most common among arthritis, hypertension, diabetes, asthma, heart disease, depression and Alzheimer disease. Stressing upon the need to start planning for demographic transition, there will be multiple vulnerabilities faced by the aged in India, especially in terms of health, income as well as social and psychological aspects. However, elderly care is predicted to soon become a major concern for developing countries like India. Geriatric care management integrates health care and psychological care with other needed services such as housing, home care services, nutritional services, assistance with activities of daily living, socialization progress as well as financial and legal planning. The phenomenon of population aging is becoming a major concern for the policy makers all over the world both for developed and developing countries.

Under these circumstances, it gives us immense pleasure to bring out this volume on old age care, development and role of Social Work. This issue is predominantly covering papers centred on the Old age care, management and the issues connected with North East and parts of India. Here we have incorporated 15 papers written by the academicians, scholars and practitioners from different parts of India.

This book has been divided into three sections. Section-I concentrates Old age aspects, programmes and policies, Section-II deals with Old age issues, limitations and problems and Section-III focuses on Elderly Care and Social Work intervention.

Section-I Concentrates Old age Aspects, Programmes and Policies consisting of five chapters.

'Summit (various aspect of aging)' paper jointly preparde by Apurba Saha and Angshu Lama tries to focus on the course of lifetime of a human being and takes up various role performances to play depending upon its age and prevailing societal norms and cultural heritage.

The paper of Subhabrata Dutta on 'Decaying Age: Problems and Policies' highlight International and national efforts have been directed for addressing the problems of older persons by adopting appropriate policies and measures such as Government of India's support in providing financial assistance to the older persons in the form of tax rebate concession in railway tickets, higher percentage of interest rate in bank and postal deposits in the name of 'senior saving schemes' etc.

Sushama Mukherjee develops a paper on 'Old Age Homes (OAHs) in India and Bangladesh: An Analysis of Health Conditions of the Elderly People' presents the conditions prevailing at the old age homes in Kolkata and Dhaka through case study method. She also suggests measures for the improvement of the existing conditions of the different old age homes.

The paper on "Elderly and Livelihood" by Ritwika Rajendra & Pranita Ghalay highlights the SHGs as an instrument for livelihood for elderly women. The paper also discusses the feelings of the elderly people about old age and the role of SHGs as a mechanism for income generation activities for the elderly people

The paper, jointly authored by Md Abdul Ahad Borbhuiya and Azmal Hussain on 'Role of Panchayat for Implementing Indira Gandhi National Old Age Pension Scheme: A Case Study of Katigorah GP, Cachar, Assam' attempts to find out the progress and target of old age scheme at field and to assess ground realities with regard to coverage, identification procedure, selection and sanctioning of cases.

Section-II deals with Old age issues, limitations and problems consisting of five chapters.

The joint paper on "Health Issues of Older Persons" by Dipak Sarkar & others tries to focus the effects on mental health of the older persons in India along with some recommendations.

'Mental Disorders among Older Adults: Identifying Risk Factors and Remedial Measures', paper prepared by Surajit Kar focuses the identification criteria of mental disorder among older adults and their different causes, risk factors and different psychological interventions to deal effectively with these stresses.

The paper on 'Crimes against the Senior Citizens of the Nation' by Jyoti Singh & Srishti Dey highlights the present scenario where the crimes against the elderly are on rise, the possible causes and solutions to India's most recent contemporary problem.

The paper on, "Violence against Older Women: Consequences and Preventive Measures" by Suraj Sharma, Nitul Das and Seema R. Nambiar attempts to deal with the causes and consequences of violence against older women and also throws light on the preventive measures that can be taken into the policies which has to be implemented at national, institutional and community levels.

The paper of Jayanta Thakuria, Meisuangdai Gonmei & Dipak Sarkar on 'National and International Organizations Working for Older Persons' aims to study the importance of National and International Organizations working for Older Persons.

Section-III focuses on Elderly Care and Social Work intervention consisting of five chapters.

'Geriatric Social Work Practice: A Case Study of an Elderly Woman Tea Plantation Worker' jointly prepared by Barsha Kalita and Kaivalya T. Desai attempts to understand the issues faced by an elderly woman in tea plantations through a detailed case study. Further it presents an example of geriatric social work practice in tea plantations.

The paper on 'Scope of Social Work Intervention for Geriatric Cancer with Reference to a Rural South Assam Cancer Care Setting' by Amit Das attempts to know the clinical and other psychosocial domains associated with aged cancer patients and also to know the scope of Social Work Intervention.

Viveni H. Yeptho, Yhunsille Seb & Amit Das prepared a paper on 'Challenges of Indian Elderly People and Scope of Social Work Intervention' focuses the welfare of the aged in Indian society through Social Work Intervention.

In the paper on 'Elderly, their Problems and Legislative Initiatives: In Search of Social Work Intervention' by Sukumar Pal, Debotosh Sinha and Sudipta Biswas suggests a number of measures as a part of social work profession for better condition of elderly and our society too.

Sabina Begum Ahmed on her paper on 'Health Care Services Provided to Elderly: A Case Study of Jeevan Deep Senior Citizen's Home, Cachar' examines the socio-economic background, the health problems and its consequences of the elderly. This paper also discusses the problems faced by the organisation for providing health care services to the elderly residing at the Jeevan Deep Senior Citizen's Home located in Silchar, Assam.

In completing writing of this volume, the authors acknowledge, all the faculty members of the Department of Social Work, Assam University, Silchar. We also acknowledge all the chapter contributors. We are indebted to National Institute of Social Defense, Ministry of Social Justice and Empowerment, Government of India for their kind assistance to organize a national seminar on this subject. We are thankful to Concept Publications, New Delhi for their interest and Co-operation in publishing this volume.

Subhabrata Dutta
Ritwika Rajendra

Section-I:
Old age Aspects, Programmes and Policies

1

"The Summit"

(Various Aspects of Aging)

Apurba Saha and *Angshu Lama*

Introduction

Growing old is a biological process and it occurs naturally to all living organisms. Human being is also not an exception to it. When a human baby is born, it grows, attains its childhood, adulthood and finally becomes old and ultimately dies, which is inevitable and nature of law. But the process of aging is a biological phenomenon; it is very much conditional to or associated with various social factors, cultural values, norms and regulations to a great extent. So during the course of lifetime of a human being, he/she takes up various role performances to play depending upon its age and prevailing societal norms and cultural heritage.

It is a phase of life cycle characterized by its own developmental issues, many of which are concerned with loss of physical ability and mental acuity, friends and loved ones, status and power. At the same time, old age is associated with the accumulation of power and wisdom and the opportunity to pass that on to future generation. It can be termed as the second childhood because an aged person needs the same amount of care and attention as the child. The concept of "old" has changed drastically over the years. Myths and stereotypes of aging have long obscured our understanding of the aged and the process of aging. People can be considered old because of certain changes in their activities or social roles.

The aging process happens during an individual's lifespan. Many human abilities peak before age 30, while other abilities continue to grow through life. The great majority of those over age 65 today are healthy, happy and fully independent. In spite of this, some individuals begin to experience changes that are perceived as signs of deterioration or decline.

Concepts of Aging

Aging: Aging is a natural phenomenon that refers to changes occurring throughout the life span and result in differences in structure and function between the youthful and elder generation.

Old Age: Old age is defined as being 60 years or older because that is the age when most of the people have been able to retire.

Gerontology: Gerontology is the study of aging and includes science, psychology and sociology.

Geriatrics: A relatively new field of medicine specialising in the health problems of advanced age.

Social Aging: Refers to the social habits and roles of individuals with respect to their culture and society. As social aging increases individual usually experience a decrease in meaningful social interactions.

Biological Aging: Refers to the physical changes in the body systems during the later decades of life. It may begin long before the individual reaches chronological age 65.

Cognitive Aging: Refers to decreasing ability to assimilate new information and learn new behaviours and skills.

Glimpse of Aging

The world's population is growing—and aging in most developing countries, are projected to increase the population aged 65 and over to the point in 2050 when it will be 2.5 times that of the population ages 0-4. In 1950, there were 131 million people aged 65+. According to United Nations Population Division estimates for mid-2010, there were 523 million aged 65+. That is, of course, quite a change. The UN also projects that, for the first time in history, the 65+ population is projected to exceed the 0-4 population during that same five-year period, rising from 601 million in 2015 to 714 million in 2020, although precisely when that happens will depend on how fast birth rates in developing countries decline.

According to Population Census 2011, there are nearly 104 million elderly persons (aged 60 years or above) in India; 53 million females and 51 million males. India's population is likely to increase by 60 per cent between 2000 and 2050, but the number of elders, who have attained 60 years of age, will shoot up by 360 per cent. India has around 104 million elderly at present and the number is expected to increase to 323 million, constituting 20 per cent of the total population, by 2050 [United Nations

Population Fund (UNFPA) and Help Age International 2012]. The per cent of literates among elderly persons increased from 27 per cent in 1991 to 44 per cent in 2011. The literacy rates among elderly females (28%) is less than half of the literacy rate among elderly males (59%). (MOSPI, 2016)

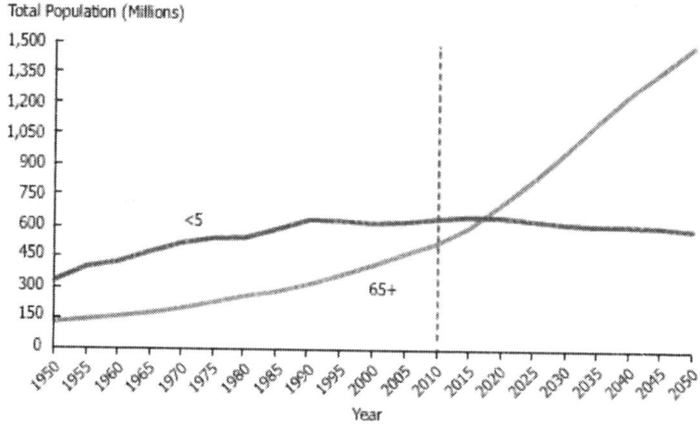

World population (Population Reference Bureau) **Population Ages 65+: 574,356,003**

Approximately 70 per cent of the elderly population is illiterate and their earning capacity in the past (during their adult years) was limited and they depended upon some productive labour work outside home for their survival. The number of people aged 80 and above, which presently are 9,249 will increase to 44,218 by 2050. Of the total number of elderly, about 83 per cent men were married and only 40 per cent women. Around three-fourths of the elderly live in rural areas, of which 48 per cent are women and 55 per cent of them are widows. Nearly 70 per cent of rural elderly are dependent on others, and their health problems increase with age. Most common disability among the aged persons was locomotor disability and visual disability as per Census 2011.

The Global Report on Aging in the 21st Century (2012) reinforces the observations made in India that there is multiple discrimination experienced by older persons, particularly older women, including in access to jobs and healthcare, subjection to abuse, denial of the right to own and inherit property, and lack of basic minimum income and social security (UNFPA & HelpAge International, 2012).

The state of Kerala which had 11 per cent of the elderly population in 2001 is expected to have 18 per cent by the year 2026, with an absolute number of around seven million elderly. On the other hand, Uttar Pradesh in 2001 had only six per cent and will have around 10 per cent elderly population in 2026. Though the proportion of the elderly population in Uttar Pradesh is smaller than in Kerala, the absolute number of elderly in Uttar Pradesh is expected to be thrice that of Kerala. Both the share and size of elderly population is increasing over time. From 5.6 per cent in 1961 the proportion has increased to 8.6 per cent in 2011. For males it was marginally lower at 8.2 per cent, while for females it was 9.0 per cent. As regards rural and urban areas, 71 per cent of elderly population resides in rural areas while 29 per cent is in urban areas. The old-age dependency ratio climbed from 10.9 per cent in 1961 to 14.2 per cent in 2011 for India as a whole. For females and males, the value of the ratio was 14.9 per cent and 13.6 per cent in 2011. (MOSPI, 2016)

Theories of Aging

A number of theories related to aging process have been described. These theories are grouped into three broad categories:

• Biological Theories

Biological theories attempt to explain the physical process of aging, including molecular and cellular changes in the major organ systems and the body's ability to function adequately and resist disease. They also attempt to explain why people age differently and what factors affect longevity and the body's ability to resist disease.

(i) Genetic Theory: According to genetic theory, aging is involuntarily inherited process that operates over time to alter cellular or tissue structures. This theory suggests that life span and longevity changes are predetermined. The development of free radicals, collagen and lipofuscin in the aging body provide some evidence for this theory and the proposition that error or mutation occurs at the molecular and cellular level.

(ii) Wear-and-Tear Theory: This theory believes that the body wears out on a scheduled basis. Free radicals, which are the waste products of metabolism, accumulate and cause damage to important biological structures. This free radicals cause DNA damage, cross linkage of collagen and the accumulation of age pigments.

(iii) Environmental Theory: According to this theory, factors in the environment (e.g. industrial carcinogens, sunlight, trauma and infection) bring about changes in the aging process. Although these factors are known to accelerate aging, the impact of the environment is a secondary rather than a primary factor in aging.

(iv) Immunity Theory: The immunity theory describes an age-related decline in the immune system. As people age their ability to defend against foreign organisms decreases, resulting in susceptibility to diseases such as cancer and infection. Along with the diminished immune function, a rise in the body's autoimmune response occurs, leading to the development of autoimmune diseases such as rheumatoid and allergies to food and environmental agents.

(v) Neuroendocrine Theory: This theory proposes that aging occurs because of a slowing of the secretion of certain hormones that have an impact on reactions regulated by the nervous system. This is most clearly demonstrated in the pituitary gland, thyroid, adrenals and the glands of reproduction.

A. Psychological Theories

Psychosocial theories focus on social and psychological changes that accompany advancing age, as opposed to the biological implications of anatomical deterioration. Several theories have attempted to describe how attitudes and behaviour in the early phases of life affect people's reactions during the late phase.

i. **Personality Theory**: This theory addresses aspects of psychological growth without delineating specific tasks or expectations of older adults. Some evidence suggests that personality characteristics in old age are highly correlated with early life characteristics. In extreme old age, however, people show greater similarity in certain characteristics, probably because of similar declines in biological functioning and societal opportunities.

ii. **Erikson's Stage of Ego Integrity**: This developmental theory identifies tasks that must be accomplished at each of the eight stages of life. The last stage of development involves reflection about one's life and accomplishments. The result of resolving this conflict between ego integrity and despair is wisdom.

iii. **Life Review**: A universal process of examination and reintegration of memories, giving meaning to life and preparing one for death by relieving anxiety and fear.

iv. **Stability of Personality**: One's personality is established by early adulthood and remains fairly stable yet adaptable (rather than a developmental progression over life span). Radical changes in personality in old age may be indicative of brain disease.

B. Socio-cultural theories:

Socio-cultural theories of aging are described as follows:

i. **Disengagement Theory:** I(t describes the process if withdrawal by older adults from societal roles and responsibilities. According to this theory, this withdrawal process is predictable, systematic, inevitable and necessary for the proper functioning of a growing society. Older adults were said to be happy when social contacts diminished and responsibilities were assumed by a younger generation. The benefit to the older adult is thought to be in providing time for reflecting on life's accomplishments and for coming to terms with unfulfilled expectations. The benefit to society is thought to be an orderly transfer of power from old to young.

ii. **Activity Theory**: In direct opposition to the disengagement theory is the activity theory of aging, which holds that the way to age successfully is to stay active. Social integration is the prime factor in determining psychosocial adaptation in later life. Social integration refers to how the aging individual is included and takes part in the life and activities of his or her society. This theory holds that the maintenance of activities is important to most people as a basis for deriving and sustaining, satisfaction, self-esteem and health.

iii. **Continuity Theory:** This theory is also known as the developmental theory, is a follow-up to the disengagement and activity theories.

   It emphasizes the individual's previously established coping abilities and personal character traits. A person who has enjoyed the company of others and active social life will continue to enjoy this lifestyle into old age.

Various Aspects of Aging

A. Biological Aspects of Aging: Individuals are unique in their physical and psychological aging processes, as influenced by their predisposition or resistance to illness, the effects of their external environment and behaviours, their exposure to trauma, infections and past diseases adopted during their life span. As the individual ages, there is a quantitative loss of cells and changes in many of the enzymatic activities within cells, resulting in a diminished responsiveness to biological demands made on the body. The biological changes that occur with the aging process includes:

i. **Skin:** One of the most dramatic changes that occur in aging is the loss of elastic in the skin. This effect, as well as changes in collagen, causes aged skin to wrinkle and sag. Fat redistribution results in a loss of the subcutaneous cushion of adipose tissue. Fewer blood vessels to the skin result in a slower rate of healing.

ii. **Cardiovascular System:** The aging heart is characterized by modest hypertrophy with reduced ventricular compliance and diminished cardiac output. This results in a decrease in response to work demands and some diminishment of blood flow to the brain, kidneys, liver, and muscles. Heart rate also slows with time.

iii. **Respiratory System:** Thoracic expansion is diminished by an increase in fibrous tissue and loss of elastic. Pulmonary vital capacity decreases, and the amount of residual air increases.

iv. **Musculoskeletal System**: Skeletal aging involving the bones, muscles, ligaments, and tendons probably generates the most frequent limitations on activities of daily living experienced by aging individuals. The elders are particularly vulnerable to osteoporosis. Individual muscle fibres become thinner and less elastic with age.

v. **Gastrointestinal System:** In the oral cavity, the teeth show a reduction in dentine production. There are some loss of bone peristalsis in the stomach and intestines, and gastric acid production decreases. Levels of intrinsic factor may also decrease, resulting in vitamin B12 mal-absorption in some aging individuals. Motility slowdown of the large intestine, combined with poor dietary habit, dehydration, lack of exercise, and some medications, may give rise to problems with constipation.

vi. **Endocrine System:** A decrease level of thyroid hormones causes a lowered basal metabolic rate. Decreased amounts of adrenocorticotropic hormone may result in less efficient stress response. Impairments in glucose tolerance are evident in aging individuals. The glucose clearance abnormalities and insulin resistance in older people may be related to many factors other than biological aging (e.g. obesity, family history of diabetes) and may be influenced substantially by diet or exercise.

vii. **Genitourinary System:** Age-related declines in renal function occur because of a steady attrition of nephrons and sclerosis within the glomeruli over time. Vascular changes affect blood flow to the kidneys and results in reduced glomerular filtration and tubular function. Elderly people are prone to develop the syndrome of inappropriate anti-diuretic hormone secretion, and levels of blood urea nitrogen and creatinine may be elevated slightly.

In men, enlargement of the prostate gland is common as aging occurs. Prostatic hypertrophy is associated with an increased risk for urinary retention and may also be a cause of urinary incontinence.

viii. **Immune System:** Aging results in changes in both cell-mediated and antibody-mediated immune responses. There is evidence of an increase in various auto-antibodies as a person ages, increasing the risk of autoimmune disorders.

ix. **Nervous System:** With aging, there is an absolute loss of neurons, which correlates with decreases brain weight of about 10 per cent by the age of 90. (Murray & Zentner, 2001) Gross morphological examination reveals gyral atrophy in the frontal, temporal, and parietal lobes, widening of the sulci; and ventricular enlargement. There are greater loss of cells in the cerebellum, the locus ceruleus, the substantia nigra, and olfactory bulbs, accounting for some of the more characteristic aging behaviours such as mild gait disturbances, sleep disruptions, and decreased smell and taste perception. Some of the age-related changes within the nervous system may be due to alterations in the neurotransmitter release, uptake, turnover, catabolism, or receptor functions.

x. **Sensory System**

- **Vision:** Vision acuity begins to decrease in mild-life. Presbyopia (blurred near vision) is the standard marker of aging of the eye. It is caused by a loss of elasticity of the crystalline lens, and results in compromised accommodation. Cataract also may be developed. The colour of the iris may fade, and the pupil may become irregular in shape. A decrease in production of secretions by the lacrimal glands may cause dryness and result in increased irritation and infection. The pupil may become constricted, requiring an increase in the amount of light needed for reading.
- **Hearing**: Hearing changes significantly with the aging process. Gradually over time, the ear loses its sensitivity to discriminate sounds because of damage to the hair cells of the cochlea.
- **Taste and Smell**: Taste sensitivity decreases over the life span. Sensitivity to sweet and salty tastes is diminished. The deterioration of olfactory bulbs is accompanied by loss of smell acuity.

- **Touch and Pain**: Organized sensory nerve receptors on the skin continue to decrease throughout the life span; thus, the touch threshold increases with age. The ability to feel pain also decreases in response to these changes, and the ability to perceive and interpret painful stimuli changes.

xi. **Cognitive Changes:** Some structural and physiological changes within the brain associated with cognitive impairment, such as reduction in the number of cells, changes in neurotransmitter levels occur in older adults both with and without cognitive impairment. Symptoms of cognitive impairments are disorientation, loss of language skills, loss of ability to calculate, and poor judgement.

B. Psychological Aspects of Aging

i. **Memory Functioning:** Short term memory deteriorates with age because of poorer sorting strategies. Long term memory does not show similar changes. However, well educated, mentally active people do not exhibit the same decline in memory functioning as their age peers who lack similar opportunities to flex their minds. The time required for memory scanning is longer for both recent and remote recall among older people. This can sometimes be attributed to social or health factors but it also occur because of certain normal physical changes associated with aging.

ii. **Intellectual Functioning:** Crystallized abilities or knowledge acquired in the course of the socialization process, tend to remain stable over the adult life span. Fluid abilities or abilities to involve in solving novel problems, tend to decline gradually from young to old adulthood. Intellectual abilities of older people do not decline but do become obsolete.

iii. **Learning Ability:** The ability to learn is not diminished by age. Studies, however, have shown that some aspects of learning do change with age. Ability to learn continues throughout life, although strongly influenced by interests, activity, motivation, health, and experience. Adjustments do need to be made in teaching methodology and time allowed for learning.

iv. **Adaptation to the Tasks of Aging**

- **Loss and Grief**: Individual experience losses from the very beginning of life. By the time individuals reach their 60s and 70s they have experienced numerous losses and mourning has become a lifelong process. Grief is cumulative, this can result in bereavement overload, which has been implicated in the predisposition to depression in the elderly.

- **Attachment to Others**: Many studies have confirmed the importance of interpersonal relationship at all stages in the life cycle. This need for attachment is consistent with the activity theory of aging that correlates the importance of social integration with successful adaptation in later life.
- **Maintenance of Self-identity**: Self-concept and self-image appear to remain stable over time. There are certain factors that favour good psychosocial adjustment in later life as family relationship, maturity of ego defences, absence of alcoholism and absence of depressive disorder. The elderly have a strong need for and remarkable capability of retaining a persistent self-concept in the faces of the many changes that contribute to instability in later life.
- **Dealing with Death:** Death anxiety among the aging is apparently more of a myth than a reality. Various investigations who have worked with dying persons report that it is not death itself, but abandonment, pain and confusion that are feared. What many desire most is someone to talk with, to show them their life's meaning is not shattered merely because they are about to die.

C. Socio-cultural Aspects of Aging

- Old age brings many important socially induced changes, some of which have the potential for negative effect on both the physical and mental well-being of older persons.
- Elderly people in virtually all cultures share some basic needs and interests. They want protection from hazards and release from the weariness of everyday tasks. They want to be treated with the respect and dignity that is deserving of individuals who have reached this pinnacle in life and they want to die with the same respect and dignity.
- The aged have had a special status in society. In some cultures, the aged are the most powerful, the most engaged and the most respected members of the society. The aged are awarded a position of honour in cultures that places emphasis on family cohesiveness.
- Many negative stereotypes colour the perspective on aging. Ideas that elderly individuals are always tired or sick, slow and forgetful,

isolated and lonely, unproductive and angry determine the way younger individuals relate to the elderly in the society.

- Assisted living centers, retirement apartment complexes and even entire retirement communities intended solely for individuals over age 50 are becoming more and more common. It is important for elderly individuals to feel part of an integrated group. This phenomenon provides additional corroboration for the activity theory of aging and the importance of attachment to others.
- Employment is another area in which the elderly experience discrimination. Although compulsory retirement has been virtually eliminated, discrimination still exists in hiring and promotion practices. Many employers are not eager to retain or hire older workers. It is difficult to determine how much of the failure to hire and promote results from discrimination based on age alone and how much of it is related to a realistic and fair appraisal of the aged employee's ability and efficiency.
- The status of the elderly may improve with time and as their numbers increase with the aging of the "baby boomers". As older individuals gain political power, the benefits and privileges designed for the elderly will increase.

3. Sexual Aspects of Aging

Sexuality and the sexual needs of elderly people are frequently misunderstood, condemned, ridiculed, repressed and ignored. Negative stereotyped notions concerning sexual interest and activity of the elderly are common. Some of these include ideas that older people have no sexual interests or desires, that they are sexually undesirable or that they are too fragile or too ill to engage in sexual activity. These cultural stereotypes undoubtedly play a large part in the misperception many people hold regarding sexuality of the aged. There is no inherent reason why individuals should not enjoy an active sexual life well into late adulthood.

(a) Physical changes associated with sexuality: Many of the changes in sexuality that occurs in later years are related to the physical changes that are taking place at that time of life.

i. Changes in women:

- Menopause begins anytime during the 40s or early 50s. There is a gradual decline in the functioning of the ovaries and the subsequent production of estrogens. The walls of the vagina become thin and inelastic, the vagina itself shrinks in both width and length and the amount of the lubrication decreases.

- Orgiastic uterine contraction may become spastic resulting in painful penetration, vaginal burning, pelvic aching or irritation on urination. In some women, the pain becomes severe resulting in avoidance of intercourse.
- Other symptoms of menopause include hot flashes, night sweats, sleeplessness, irritability, mood swings, migraine headaches, urinary incontinence and weight gain.
- Some menopausal women elect to take hormone replacement therapy for relief of these symptoms. However, some women choose not to take the hormone because of an increased risk of breast cancer and endometrial cancer.

ii. Changes in men:

- Testosterone production declines gradually over the years, beginning between ages 40 and 60. A major change resulting from this hormone reduction is that erections occur more slowly and require more direct genital stimulation to achieve.
- There may be a modest decrease in the firmness of the erection in men older than age 60.
- The volume of ejaculate gradually decreases and the force of ejaculation lessens.
- The testes become somewhat smaller, but most men continue to produce viable sperm well into old age.
- Prolonged control over ejaculation in middle-aged and elderly men may bring increased sexual satisfaction for both partners.
- Coital frequency in early marriage and the overall quantity of sexual activity between age 20 and 40 correlate significantly with frequency patterns of sexual activity during aging.
- Although sexual activity appears to decline with age, studies show that significant numbers of elderly men and women have active and satisfying sex lives well into their 80s.

Conclusion

Rapid expansion of older adult numbers in the world population is one of the crucial demographic changes of present time. In India, as well as in other countries across the world, the population is aging very rapidly. The life expectancy level has increased drastically from pre- to post-independence and in current context. The projected numbers may also increase over the coming two decades. The growing trends of older adults will likely pose new societal challenges for providing this group with health care, financial assistance, and social and emotional support. The aging population trend, in conjunction with social and economic trends, is also ushering in new concerns about changing family values, living arrangements, and lifestyles. Family care giving for older adult relatives is also vital concern due to changing pattern in our family and marriage system.

The older adult has many sides, making it a complex, yet pleasant process which we all experience. The physiological, economic, emotional and interpersonal aspects influence the social functioning and well-being of individuals in different ways. In view of the youth and middle-aged, old age perhaps the end of journey and a remote phase of life. However, the recognition that population are aging has motivated widespread public attention on the implications of the changing demographic structure, with much of the focus centering around the welfare and well-being of the elderly.

Though, older adults are vulnerable to health problems due to several factors such as mental and neurocognitive disorders, social isolation, feelings of disconnectedness & loss of relatives, neurocognitive impairment and altered decision making, chronic physical illnesses, and physical and psychological pain. But, Aging now needs to be understood as a universal phenomenon of growth and development and not as a period of disease and disability.

Care of the aging individual presents one of the greatest challenges, with the growing of the aging population the challenge will progress in future. Individual experience many changes as they age as well as experience many losses, potentially leading to bereavement overload. Caring for elderly individuals requires a special kind of inner strength and compassion.

REFERENCES

Elderly in India, (2016). Ministry of Statistics and Programme Implementation, Social Statistics Division, Government of India.

Gelder, M., Harrison, P., (2006.). *Shorter Oxford Textbook Psychiatry*. 5th ed. New York: Oxford University Press Inc.

Sharma, S., Chadda, R.K., (1997). *Essential of Psychiatry*. 1st ed. New Delhi: Mehta Offset Works.

Stuart, G.W., (2011). *Principles and Practice of Psychiatric Nursing*. 9th ed. St. Louise: Elsevier.

Townsend, M.C., (2010). *Psychiatric Mental Health Nursing*. 7th edition. New Delhi; Jaypee Brother Medical Publishers (P) Ltd.

World Health Organisation. World population aging. [Serial online] 2002[cited 20th Nov 2013]. Available from: http://www.nia.nih.gov/

2
Decaying Age: Problems and Policies

Subhabrata Dutta

Introduction

Ageing is a natural phenomenon. A man after birth passes through a long-drawn cycle process of growth, decay and death. So it is an inevitable phase in the life of every man. It is an unalterable, universal and inescapable reality of human life. No man can avoid it. In the olden days when there was the prevalence of joint families, old age had been accepted as a normal thing and care in later life had been a point and collective responsibility. But old age began to appear as a human problem along with the rapid urbanization transformation in family values and number of other factors leading to nuclear families and massive migration in search of better employment. Old age becomes a matter of critical concern because of the rising level of life expectancy due to scientific advancement and medical improvement. Every society in both developed and developing countries has a significant population of elderly people. It is a global matter and India is a no exception. The population dynamics have been changing with average longevity passing 60 years of age and above. The pace of population ageing in India had been passing through a process of fluctuation from 1901 to 1961. After 1961, the number of ageing population has been registering a rising trend. The growth in the older population with continue to rise during this 21st century.

Indian Scenario

In India, as per 2011 population census, the percentage of population aged 60 and above is 8.6 and it is projected to rise to 20 per cent by 2050. India stands second of China today in respect of older persons. The scenario of growing elderly population has demographically definite repercussion on India's population. Graying population in a developing country like India poses a serious challenge before the Government, both Central and State and above all to the society. Old age has involved some problems such as financial, health, psychological and several other types of challenges. A critical challenge surfaces in the demographic history of India.

Table 2.1: Percentage of aged population of 60 years and above in India

Years	Percentage of aged population %
1901	5.06
1919	5.22
1921	5.37
1931	5.09
1941	5.66
1951	5.43
1961	5.63
1971	5.97
1981	6.42
1991	6.55
2001	7.70
2011	8.6

Source: Office of the Registrar General and Census Commissioner, India.

Table 2.1 shows that the national graying population growth for the period from 1901 to 1951 shows a slight rising trend with minor degrees of change. But the older population growth for the period from 1951 to 2011 registers a steady increasing trend.

Another disturbing area of ageing in India is urban-rural variation and male-female variation. In India, the aged population living in rural areas is higher and larger than those living in urban areas. Secondly, there are more elderly women than older men because elderly women have a greater longevity than the older males have. Elderly women generally live more than their male counterparts. Table 2.2 shows the higher percentage of aged women than the older males.

Table 2.2: Higher Percentage of aged females than aged males

Years	Percentage of aged females (%)	Percentage of aged males (%)
1901	5.59	4.55
1911	5.65	4.81
1921	5.70	5.04
1931	5.35	4.86
1941	5.91	5.43
1951	5.66	5.21
1961	5.80	5.46
1971	5.99	5.96
1981	6.50	6.35
1991	6.66	6.45
2001	7.86	7.55
2011		

Source: Office of the Registrar General and Census Commissioner, India.

Main Problems

A number of studies have identified various problems that the older persons face during the twilight zone of their life. Some of the major problems confronted by the old persons are related to financial insecurity, health problems, psychological problems and physical abuse. Again these problems vary from one person to another depending on a number of factors, such as composition of family, attitude of the younger generation, financial status, liabilities and physical and mental requirement.

Economic Insecurity

Economic insecurity is one of the major problems faced by the elderly people and the elderly women face their problem more acutely. The financial insecurity is due to the decrease in income and the ailing elderly people feel the pinch of economic insecurity more severely. The older persons are gradually depending upon the inmates of the family for their sustenance. Older persons with inadequate resources are gradually becoming burden on the family and the society. This problem may be aggravated if the elderly persons wowed transfer their movable and immovable property in the name of their sons and daughters. Different empirical studies have shown that the majority of elderly respondents had cited their financial problem as their main problem. The majority of the aged women both in rural and urban areas have suffered more acutely from the economic insecurity. But the older persons of the different families are too some extent free from this sense of financial insecurity.

Health Problems

Many studies have shown that health problem of the elderly people has been recognized as a more serious problem of all problems confronted by them. Due to the change of surroundings and decline of physical vitality, health problems arise. Since the physical strength declines with the advancement of age, older persons are becoming more vulnerable to different diseases. Various ailments threaten their health and safety. In transitional economies like India, malnutrition coupled with poverty and declining vitality play a vital role in precipitation of various diseases. Some of the common ailments from which the aged persons suffer are poor eyesight, cold and cough, anemia, arthritis, dwindling hearing capacity. Many other lifestyle diseases such as diabetes, cardiac ailment, dementia etc effect the elderly people. Different studies have revealed that majority of the elderly population of all segments of society suffer from nutritional deficiency

Apart from physical ailments, the elderly suffer from various psychological and emotional diseases. Feeling of loneliness and emptiness are some of the major psycho-emotional problems. A feeling of emptiness produces sometimes suicidal tendencies among the frail elderly people. A feeling of depression and despair always haunts them.

Elderly Abuse

Another major disturbing problem is elder abuse. Older persons are abused, neglected and exploited in various ways by family, friends, spouses, care-providers, legal guardians. Physical debility and social isolation render the elderly people more vulnerable than other members of society. Different news reports in both print and electronic, course cases shows that abuse and neglect elderly people is emerging as a wide spread serious problem. This problem is all pervasive in all sections of society and in both rural and urban sections.

International and National Initiatives

In 1982, U.N. General Assembly had organized the historic World Assembly on Ageing with a view to creating awareness about the developmental and humanitarian significance of the older persons of the world. Further, the General Assembly in 1992 declared the year 1999 as "International Year of the Older Persons'. Moreover, the General Assembly adopted United Nations eighteen principles in favour of the older persons.

In appropriate recognition of the UN declaration of "The International Year of Older Persons' (1999), the Union Government of India formulated the 'National Policy on Older Persons' in January, 1999. In order to overcome various problems and challenges faced by the elderly people, a large number of initiatives have been launched by the successive Governments, both Central and States to ensure social justice, protection and provision for financial assistance. Another important legislative initiative had already been taken in 2007, regarding the 'Maintenance and Welfare of Parents in the Senior Citizens Act, 2007'. This legislation aims at providing more effective provisions for the welfare of parents and senior citizens, guaranteed and recognized in the Constitution of India.

The Central Government has provided some financial assistance to the older persons in the form of tax rebates, concessions in railway tickets and in paying a higher percentage of interest to the Bank and postal deposits such as 'Senior Saving Scheme'. The West Bengal Government has introduced a number of financial schemes for helping the poor elderly people. A large number of poor elderly people have enjoyed various pension schemes under the 'National Social Assistance Programme', such as Indira Gandhi Old Age Pension Scheme, Indira Gandhi National Widow Pension Scheme, Indira Gandhi National Disability Pension Scheme. Under the Schemes, only 21 lakh and 31 thousand persons of West Bengal are entitled to these national pension schemes. In order to expand the pension coverage, the West Bengal Government has introduced a special scheme "Bangla Special Allowance Scheme (Balglar Vishesh Bhata Prakalpa)" (*Source*: Bartaman Patrika – P-I, dt. 22.02.2018). Under this scheme, people aged between 60 years to 79 years, will be entitled to receive Rs. 400 per month. Older persons above 80 will be entitled to receive Rs. 1000 per month. But the beneficiaries should belong to B.P.L. Category. These schemes are not available for all. This is one major limitation of the policy.

Recommendations and Suggestions Regarding Policies for Older Persons

Universal Pension Scheme

The ratio of the geriatric population is on the increase all-over the world.

The problems and challenges faced by elder people in all sectors are varied and of perplexing nature. In order to cope with the emerging challenges, care services in later life, health care services, physical protection against elderly abuse, and financial support need to be developed both qualitatively and quantitatively. The writer is in favour of 'introducing universal pension scheme' which is very successfully implemented in many low-income countries and transitional economics such as Botswana, Bolivia. Universal social pension can be an effective tool for giving financial security to the elderly people.

Health Care Services

Health care services ought to be easily accessible to all sections of the populace. Oder persons are more in need of health care services. But it is an area where the elderly people are at the risk of danger. In India, expenses for health care services, particularly at private level, are exorbitant. Many studies have shown that a large number of people in India, an average of 25 per cent of Indians, are becoming impoverished because of medical expenses.

Community Health Awareness Scheme is one of the viable options for protecting the people from catastrophic health expenditure. This scheme had already been gaining popularity, especially in Africa. This scheme has become effective for protecting a considerable portion of the African population, for example, Rwanda where more than 45 per cent of its population is covered.

Care in later life

It is an important aspect for the welfare of the elderly people because older people are the largest group of users of care services. Formal or institutional care services are very poor at present for the elderly. Residential and nursing home care remains a key provision for elderly persons. The Government's responses are very poor in this respect. Informal or private care services are more of less available today. But these are not always affordable for all. Such care services are highly charged. So, the government should increase its expenditure on this sector. Otherwise older persons, particularly older women will be financially burdened for needing care and support in later life.

Social Support for the Older Persons

Family support is one of the key support-providers for the older persons. Family members and kinship relationship are the most important, first and preferred providers of social support. In the United States, more than seven million Americans provide care in later life to their family members. Such care providers in later life are best provided by Asian Americans, African Americans and Italian Americans. Secondly, another kind of social support may be available at the semi-formal level such as in clubs, churches, neighbourhoods and senior citizen centres. Well-meaning neighbours, relatives and acquaintances can play a positive role at this level. Many countries have already started building 'Senior Citizen Centres'. At these centres older persons can hold regular meeting and can performs things related to common interest – such as playing cards, opening and reading at book clubs, organizing seminars, plenary pleasure trips, holding picnics, and exercise classes. All these steps and programmes can exercise a beneficial impact upon the elderly persons at the grassroot level.

Social Work Intervention

It is a fact that Geriatric problems are multidimensional. Social work profession can play a special role in this respect. It has to face many challenges at different levels. At one level, social work profession aims at helping individuals, groups or communities to maintain a balance between needs and rights.

Social work philosophy believes is helping the clients help themselves. So, it has an extensive area of work from social reform to personal help. It can also help in the formulation of policy for the aged, in creating healthy relationship in the family, monetary assistance through formation of self-held groups (SHGs) and other income-generating activities, support and counselling at the emergency. The social worker can help the aged in different settings and environment such as care giving institutions, hospitals etc. Social workers can act as a catalytic agent in making healthcare services accessible, particularly to the low-income groups. Another important service is to sensitize the society and the community over the issues of the elderly persons. The young generations should be sensitized to look at the issues of the older persons with a positive and affirmative approach.

Gerontological Social Work

Another important step in facing the challenges of old age is the development and expansion of Gerontological Social Work. The social work profession has a definite role to play in this regard. Very few universities in India have provided courses in Gerontological social work.

Development and preparation of course curricula in keeping with the changing demands of the changed situation is essential. Finally, we hope that the social work profession will sincerely devote its time and attention to the rights, needs and demands of the graying population so that they can lead a healthy and hopeful old age. We must keep in mind: "Old is gold".

REFERENCES

Bali, A.P. (1999). *Understanding Graying People of India*, ICSSR, New Delhi.

GOI, (2011). *Situation Analysis of the Elderly in India. Central Statistics Office Ministry of Statistics & Programme Implementation*, Government of India.

GOI, (2011). *Census Report 2011*, Government of India.

Kholi, A.S., (1999). *Social Situation of Aged in India*, Anmol Publication, New Delhi.

Kumar, S., Sathyanarayana, K.M., Omer, A., (2011). *Living Arrangements of Elderly in India: Trends and Differentials. International Conference on Challenges of Population Aging in Asia*, UNFPA, New Delhi, India.

Lena, A., Ashok, K., Padma, M., Kamath, V., Kamath, A., (2009). "Health and Socio Problems of the Elderly : A Cross Sectional Study in Udupi Taluk", Karnataka. *Indian Journal of Community Medecine,* Vol. 34: 131-134.

Mane, A.B., Khandekar, S.V., Fernandez, K., (2014). "India's ageing Population: Geriatric Care Still in Infancy". *J. Gerontol Geriatr Res.,* Vol. 3,186.

Patel, V., Prince, M., (2001). "Ageing and Mental Health in a Developing Country: Who Cares? Qualitative studies from Goa, India". *Psycho Med*, Vol. 31:29-38.

Patel, A.A., (1998). "Loneliness among the Elderly: The Role Perceived Responsibility and Control", *Recent Researches in Education and Psychology*, Vol. 3 (1-2), 21-25.

Shenoy, A.S., (2014). "Social Protection and Social Welfare of Elders". *South Asia Regional Co-operation Newsletter,* 1-8.

WHO, (2002). Tufts University School of Nutrition and Policy. Keep fit for life: Meeting the nutritional needs of older persons. WHO, Geneva, Switzerland.

3

Old Age Homes (OAHs) in India and Bangladesh

An Analysis of Health Conditions of the Elderly People

Sushama Mukherjee

Introduction

Time was when the extended family rather than the nuclear was the norm. Even in many European countries in the pre-industrial times when the feudal or primarily agrarian society existed, the extended family prevailed. However, as industrialization and various allied commercial activities grew apace, men and women left their village homes and flocked to urban areas in search of new and better opportunities. This transition from the feudal society to an industrial society was characterized by a simultaneous decline and eventual disintegration of the extended family system. Society in many Asian countries including the Indian sub-continent (comprising India, Bangladesh and Pakistan) was predominantly agrarian or feudal until the second half or even the closing decades of the 20th century.

Traditional support received from family or community by the elderly is almost fading out of contemporary society. Owing to various socio-economic factors, the traditional support to the elderly is gradually changing its character. The character of supporting elderly is gradually undergoing transformation that can be attributed to various changes in social and economic arenas. The elderly are facing a host of problems rather than living in peace and with honour. Many older people are becoming dependent on family members for their daily existence. Since they have no earnings or means, deteriorating health has resulted to medical problems in old age; they are considered burdensome by family members and the society at large. The older people are sometimes forced to leave their homes and stay at old age homes. Thus, it is pertinent to understand the context of the elderly in old age homes. The elderly population is continuously increasing. As life expectancy has risen in

India and Bangladesh, the elderly population has grown simultaneously. As per the United Nations, the World population is projected to rise to 9.8 billion by 2050 from the current (7.3). During the same period, the proportion of the elderly population is estimated to increase from 0.14 per cent to 21.7 per cent. So, the problem has assumed global proportions. Like most other Indian states, West Bengal is subject to fluctuation of population ageing in India. There are 74,90,514 persons (51.4% males and 48.6% females). Bangladesh is the eighth largest and one of the most densely populated countries in the World. According to Bangladesh Bureau of statistics (2011 census), the total population of Bangladesh is 142 million out of which 7.48 per cent consists of ageing population. Ageing is a natural phenomenon forming an essential part of the long-drawn cycle of growth and decay. In earlier times, older people were given special respect and high position in society thanks to their experience and wisdom. But such values of life have been gradually eroded with the passage of time. Unfortunately, elderly are considered not as repositories of wisdom but an unsustainable burden on the society. This undesirable mindset can be attributed to the impact of factors like industrialization, urbanization, westernization, changing roles of women and the breakdown of the traditional extended family structure. We must recognize that there is now widespread discontent in the life of the elderly and they have to contend with myriad problems and difficulties. It is crystal clear that the major problems plaguing the elderly are financial insecurity, health problems and psychosocial problems like feelings of loneliness and depression. In countries like India and Bangladesh given the paucity of funds and resources, malnutrition and poverty is a very common phenomenon thing in the elderly human life. In India and Bangladesh, the context of institutional homes for the elderly is relatively new. The loneliness, the neglect and the lack of proper holistic care are rampant in many places and although most of the older people live to accept the existing environment as nobody seems to be really interested in taking care of the various needs of elderly. This sometimes leads the life of the elderly in old age homes which is a little less miserable and less unbearable. Hence, those tasked with looking after the elderly in the old age homes must make it a point to be more caring, empathetic and understand.

Research Methodology

Research Objective

The research study is intended to make a comprehensive study of the health-related problems afflicting the elderly residents at the old age homes. The specific objectives are as follows:

1. To identify factors that forces the elderly to live in old age homes in India and Bangladesh.
2. To know the health condition of the elderly residents living in old age homes.
3. To understand the role of government and non-governmental organizations (NGOs) regarding health-related problems of the older people living in old age home.

Research Questions

The present study addresses the following research questions:

1. What are the factors that lead the elderly to live in old age homes?
2. What are the problems of the elderly residents regarding their health conditions at old age homes under the study area?
3. What activities are undertaken by the government and non-governments organizations to improve the conditions of the elderly residents at the old age homes?

Database and Method of Research

With the aim to achieve the objectives, the researcher has used a comparative research design to understand the health conditions and problems faced by the elderly living in old age homes in India and Bangladesh. Further, it would also help to observe the daily life of the elderly residents of OAHs and reveal new facts about them. In addition to get an in-depth understanding about the elderly who live in old age home in Kolkata, West Bengal (India) and Dhaka (Bangladesh), the method and data of the qualitative approaches was adopted in the study. Thus, qualitative approach that include case study and focus group discussion were conducted along with descriptive ways to gather more information about the health and living conditions of the elderly residents at old age homes.

In this study, both primary and secondary data were used. Data was collected from every selected elderly resident, those who are interested to take part in the study; and also, the key informants at OAHs. The information was collected through face to face in-depth interview was used for data collection and observation was a supplementary data collection technique here and check-list for focus group discussion was also used here. Secondary data were gathered from Bangladesh Government of Social Welfare Department, West Bengal Government of Social Welfare Department, and also the secondary data have been collected from various sources, including research articles and various reports issued by various institutions and web based resources.

Study Area

The study areas, Kolkata city of West Bengal in India and Dhaka city of Bangladesh have been selected for the study. West Bengal is one of the most populous Indian states. Ranked among the countries in the World with the highest density of population Bangladesh is the eighth largest country in the World. The older people who are aged more than 60 and living in OAHs under the study area were taken for the study. The selected study area of both countries is similar from the viewpoint of language, social and cultural aspects. In Kolkata, West Bengal, India, two old age homes were randomly selected, and Dhaka Bangladesh, two homes for the aged were indiscriminately chosen.

Sample and sampling

The purposive (non-probabilistic) sampling technique had been used for selecting old age homes in both India and Bangladesh. Purposive sampling was used for selecting key informants.

Limitations of the study

The study is confined to the elderly living in old age homes in Kolkata city of India and Dhaka city of Bangladesh. It cannot be generalized on the entire aged population of both the countries. The present study is conducted through the case study method. So, the study is limited to the older people living in the old age homes in Dhaka Bangladesh and Kolkata West Bengal. However, in both the countries many old age home residents kept mum on their experience.

Findings of the Case Studies

Case Study- 1: Bayasko Punarbasan Kendra Old Age Home: Gazipur (Bangladesh)

Financially Abused by Family and Attacked by Serious Disease

Parshi Koriea (name changed) aged 85, and by religion a Christian Catholic, is an illiterate woman from Pabna, Bangladesh. Her husband who worked as a cook died 18 years ago when he was 70. Parshi had seven sons and a daughter, of whom two sons and the daughter had already died. Her five living sons, all aged between 50 and 60 are mostly illiterate and all of them are married. Parshi's father's house and in-laws' house are both in Pabna.

Following her husband's death, Parshi received her property but she had distributed it among her five sons. She also had a bank deposit to the tune of 80 thousand taka (BD) but she gave it to her eldest son. Thus, after distributing whatever she had among her children, she was afflicted with Kidney disease and her kidneys were not functioning properly. Her sons did not shoulder any responsibility for her treatment and her kidneys were operated upon with the help of a Catholic Father. As both her kidneys were not functioning, she could not return to her family life though she wanted to, because her daughters-in-law refused to take her back into the family since she was not able to work anymore and her sons also tacitly sided with their wives in this respect. So, being penniless and absolutely shelterless, she again turned to the Catholic Father who had arranged for her a shelter in the Gazipur old age home because meals and lodging are free of cost here and she can live a comparatively secure life here. She came here in 2015 and since then she has been residing here.

Parshi received the usual facilities including general medicines, clothes and other necessities at the old age home but her experience is not exactly satisfactory. She admits that she received clothes, medicines and other necessities from the old age home authorities free of cost, and that is definitely a boon for her.

But being a serious kidney patient, she needs a specialized treatment schedule and a specialized diet which were not available here. For treatment she has to depend on a Catholic Father who takes her to specialized doctors for treatment and arranges for the requisite medicines. The other serious problem is that she is the only Christian resident among the Muslim dominated old age home residents and sometimes she faces certain restrictions while performing her religious rituals. So there is a lack of mental adjustment on her part in relation to her roommates or other residents. Parshi Koriea does not find herself on the same wavelength with her roommates or other old age home residents. Indeed, she feels like a fish out of water. Her kidney disease makes it difficult for her to do any household chores and she badly needs a professional caregiver who is unavailable. Still, with no option left to return to family life, she continues living here whether she likes it or not.

Parshi Koriea used to receive the Bangladesh Government "Bayashka Bhata" of twelve hundred takas quarterly which was arranged by the Catholic Father and so she was quite aware of the government scheme. She received this aid for 8 to 9 years but it suddenly stopped and now she faces real trouble without the much-needed money. If it had still continued she would have been able to use it for specialized treatment of her kidneys and for purchasing medicines.

During her stay in this old age home for 4 years, Parshi had mixed feelings of both good experience and bad. But what causes her anguish is the fact that she can never be reunited with her family. Nobody wants her back and nobody even come to the old age home to visit her. She holds her disease responsible for her estrangement from her kin and this really makes her feel depressed and lonely. However, with nothing left, she resigns herself to her life here.

Life for Parshi Koriea is now governed by the old age home rules and regulation. She realizes that given her disease, her penniless plight and estrangement from her kin, she has no choice but to endure her life here despite the non-cooperation of or even opposition from, other residents.

Case Study-2: Bayasko Punarbasan Kendra Old Age Home: Gazipur (Bangladesh)

Victim of Poverty and Health Hazard

Farida Begum (name changed) is 72 years old. An illiterate female and by religion a Sunni Muslim, she married at early age and her husband had passed away when he was 52. She had, 3 sons and a daughter. But the daughter died when she was three and Farida's younger son died at the age of 3 months. She is left with two sons, aged 46 and 44 respectively. The older son works as a bus conductor while the youngest (one) worked as a manager of CNG Auto. Now, they have their own families.

Her spouse's death plunged Farida Begum into deep trouble as she did not have any money to look after her two sons. Although her deceased husband was a rickshaw puller by profession, he ended up being a spieler who squandered his money. So, after his death Farida was forced to work as a domestic help to raise her two (surviving) sons and lived in a rented house. But the older son, like his father took to gambling. He was unable to look after properly of his own family. Nor did her younger son earn much and so he could not take care of his mother. At present Farida is suffering from various health ailments like diabetes, hypertension and arthritis. As she is unable to afford to pay for the treatment, she had decided to stay at OAHs and she had preferred Gazipur old age home because the services provided are free of cost. In the OAHs, she could enjoy accommodation, her food and medical treatment facilities.

Farida received many facilities here. The things she received here free of cost are medicine, clothes and other daily necessities. These facilities mean a great deal to her.

But she also faces some problems here. The authorities arrange for general health check-up. But Farida suffers from several diseases like diabetes, hypertension and arthritis which are chronic requiring specialized treatment which the old age home authorities are unable to provide. Farida herself cannot afford such treatment on her own. Another problem is that the OAH authorities here cannot arrange for any professional caregivers. Farida herself has to do her own work, according to the rules in this OAH. It is very difficult for her to do so since she is a patient of arthritis and has restricted movements. She also has to share one bathroom with 9 other residents. This is a problem she has to grapple with daily. The OAH authorities allow her to go home only two times a year. Nor can her family members visit her regularly. The authorities here have strictly prohibited the use of mobile phones. So, she has very little communication with her kin. Naturally, a sense of deep loneliness and depression affects her. She is generally aloof though she has cordial relations with the other residents. Despite the problems she lives here because she has no other option than to make adjustments and accept her life here.

Farida is not aware of the schemes of the Government of Bangladesh meant for the welfare of the elderly. The old age home authorities do not (give) any information to her regarding this. But Farida thinks that some governmental help will definitely benefit her considerably.

Her problems notwithstanding, it is no doubt a good alternative shelter for Farida since it fulfils the basic necessities of her life which is something, she found impossible in her family. So, she goes on living here and will continue to do so for the rest of her life.

Case Study-3: Kalyan Ashram Old Age Home (Kolkata South) Help Age India

• Forced separation from married daughter coupled with an incapacitating illness

Sarbani Banerjee (name changed), aged 69 and professing the faith of Hinduism, lived in Duars in North Bengal, India, where both her father's and her in-laws houses were situated. After passing H.S. exam she got married to a worker in an NGO who additionally, ran a business. They have a daughter, by education graduate, who is now a housewife living in Kudghat, Kolkata (India). However, Sarbani's husband passed away in 2008 and following his death Sarbani disposed of her husband's property and with the aid of his brother she deposited the money from the sale proceeds.

Her husband being no more, Mrs. Banerjee became completely alone. Many suggested that she should live with her daughter and her daughter also asked her to reside with her. But following the common tradition, Sarbani was not willing to live in her married daughter's house; she wanted to live independently. So she decided willingly to go to a home for the aged persons and accordingly she opted for the Kolkata Kalyan Ashram Old Age Home under the auspices of Help Age India. She was admitted there in 2008 and since then she has been staying there.

In the Kalyan Ashram old age home, Mrs. Banerjee shares a four bed room with an attached bath room with three other residents. At the time of admission a deposit sum of Rs.25,000 had to be given on account of medical emergency and the amount is refundable. Her stay in this home for the elderly is entirely free of cost. In addition she enjoys the benefit of a free medical general check-up once a month. But the absence of specialized check-up is a problem for her because she regularly suffers from arthritis and for obtaining specialized treatment she has to go outside. However, there is a free physiotherapy centre in the old age home which is particularly beneficial to her. She even availed herself of it earlier but now she cannot do so because of her arthritis pain. That is why she definitely wants the facility of specialized treatment inside the old age home itself. Another facility that Sarbani likes very much is an annual tour conducted by the old age home free of cost. The food served here also seems okay to her. But the problem is that the cook here acts also as the caregiver in the old age home, there being no separate caregiver. Naturally, it is difficult for one caregiver to perform the duties of both cooking and looking after the residents at the same time and it is particularly difficult for Sarbani whose movements are severely restricted. A separate caregiver would have been really beneficial for her. Another big problem for her is the absence of a lift here. She has to go outside once a month for specialized treatment and in the absence of the lift, she is forced to use the staircase. This is, indeed, the most challenging problem for her since she can hardly move and it's now almost impossible for her to use the staircase. She maintains a cordial relationship with the other residents and in general she has established good rapport with all the residents in the OAH. Mrs. Banerjee has a Mediclaim policy which definitely stands her in good stead as regards her specialized treatment since she has been suffering from this disease since 1982. She loved to read books but now cannot read much because of her painful disease. Earlier she used to visit her daughter's home from time to time though her daughter never visited the Old age Home to see her. But now she can hardly do so because of her illness.

She is well familiar with the government schemes for the older people but cannot enjoy the benefit of any of these because nobody takes the initiative to enable her to avail herself of the schemes.

Sarbani Banerjee enjoys her independent life in this home for the elderly in the company of other roommates. The biggest problem is her arthritis that has severely restricted her movements and prevents her from enjoying her life in a way she would have liked to.

Sarbani's experience is a clear indicator that the old age home is meant not only for those who are outcasts, but also for those who come here willingly, and try to enjoy their lives in their own way with others. It can really be a good alternative refuge for the elderly who, for some reason, find themselves estranged from their kin and (hence) unable to enjoy the family environment.

Case Study-4: Shantineer Old Age Home (Baranagar, Kolkata North)

• An unfortunate victim of Property Abuse and a crippling health problem

Mrs. Renuka Saha (name changed) aged 76 years and by religion a Hindu is a resident of Baharampur, West Bengal. After passing H.S. Renuka was married to a businessman in 1962 and was leading her life as a homemaker with two sons both of whom were businessmen and married. However, unfortunately for her, her husband died in 1987 at the age of 49 and her elder son also passed away at the age of 46 in 2003.

Though Renuka's husband died early, before his death he had transferred all his property and financial assets to her. This helped her to bring up both her sons. The elder one stayed in Baharampur while the younger one came to Kolkata. Renuka stayed with her elder son but here she made the mistake of transferring all her property to her elder son. Sadly, the son died in 2003 and the property was transferred in favour of the elder daughter-in-law. The financial assets were transferred to the name of the younger son. Her elder daughter-in-law then refused to look after Renuka and drove her out of the house. She came over to her younger son but he also refused to let her stay with his family. He advised her to take shelter in the old age home. So the situation became extremely pathetic for Renuka. She was a pauper, and a victim of property abuse and neglect by the family. So she was forced to seek refuge in the Shantineer home for the aged in 2018 and has since been living there.

The Shantineer home for the aged old age home where Renuka stays consists of twenty rented flats in a housing complex at Baranagar, Kolkata and each flat has two rooms with five beds in each room with just one attached bathroom. Here Renuka stays in one bed for which she has to pay Rs.4500 per month, inclusive of meal charges. Her medical expenditure is also a burden because there is no arrangement for free medical check-up here and the medical check-up expenses are borne by Renuka herself. There is a general monitoring system on the part of the old age home authorities to take care of the necessities of residents like Renuka. There are also arrangements for a free medical check-up once in a month and an on-call ambulance service for which Renuka and other residents have to pay. She also complains about the food quality which should have been better, the lack of space inside the room and the fact that there is only one ceiling fan in each room which is certainly not enough. In this old age home, apart from the Rs.4500/- per month everything is payable by Renuka herself. This sometimes exerts tremendous pressure on Renuka's meagre finances. There are no professional caregivers here. Neither is there any arrangement for attendants. If Renuka has to engage any attendant, she will have to pay her fees. This is, indeed, her major problem because she is a patient of arthritis and without an attendant it is very difficult for her to do her own domestic chores. Still, she continues her life here maintaining a cordial relationship with the other residents here.

Renuka is completely unaware of the government welfare schemes/ policies in respect of the elderly but she says that if she had availed of them, she would have benefitted immensely. She says that even the authorities also do not know much about government welfare schemes.

Staying in the old age home is a definite financial burden on Renuka though she also deplores the neglect shown by her family members after they received her property. However she carries on with her life here where she can live with honour and dignity and comes to terms with the problems she faces here.

Renuka's life is an example of how elderly women are being exploited and neglected by their families. The old age home at least gives women like Renuka the opportunity to spend life in a somewhat dignified manner.

Major Findings and Conclusions

Important Findings of the Study

- The elderly in India and Bangladesh find themselves in a state of terrible uncertainty and, indeed, in an existential crisis owing to a combination of several factors, they are (a) erosion of long-cherished norms and values associated with extended family system, (b) the economic compulsion or financial constraints of children of elderly and the financial crunch faced by the elderly themselves, and (c) the neglect, abuse and exploitation, the elderly are subjected to by their kin.

- The major problem plaguing the elderly residents at old age homes is their health conditions. Deteriorating health that resulted to medical problems has characterized old age. The depleted finances or the paltry earnings can hardly keep pace with the spiralling prices of all essential commodities and the mounting medical bills. Thus, sheer survival becomes a tremendous challenge for the elderly in twilight years of their life. Thus, they are compelled to seek refuge in old age homes where they are assured of food, shelter and a modicum of medical aid. This kind of situation prevails in both India and Bangladesh and thus is an emerging societal issue.
- Both in India and Bangladesh, most of the residents of old age home have to remain without any specialized medical treatment. This problem has compounded by escalating medical expenses and paucity of funds, which haunts these elderly residents like a nightmare. Unfortunately, most of old age homes have no arrangements for specialized treatment. Therefore, a proper and adequate medical infrastructure should be put in place for survival and physical well-being of residents of old age home.
- Both in India and Bangladesh, the percentage of the female elderly widows are very high and thus call for special attention and urgent amelioration. Owing to their abject dependence on family financial conditions, their contributions are either non-existent or woefully inadequate thus, these hapless widows are caught up in the throes of an abysmal financial crisis. The severe health problems add to their woes. If they are to survive, they must be treated with special care and attention by providing social security. But there has been little progress in both the countries in enabling the eligible widows with widow pension benefits. Most of these female elderly widows are illiterate and are not aware of any government related schemes for the elderly. Hence, appropriate official initiatives must be taken.
- There is no denying the need for an appropriate health insurance policy as far as the senior citizens including the (homes for the elderly) residents in India and Bangladesh are concerned. A suitable health insurance policy can stand them in good stead in times of dire need. In both the countries in the surveyed old age homes, the residents stated that they do not have any health insurance policy because most of them belong to the ultra-poor level. They also have been afflicted with various diseases and so

they need to avail of some health related policy measures. In India, there is the 'Rashtriya Swasthya Bima Yojana'. This policy was launched in 2008. The eligibility criterion for this policy is to be an Indian citizen and to be below poverty level. This will provide health insurance to the family including children and dependent parents. The West Bengal government funded the 'Swasthya Sathi' scheme (2016) and announced that every family (child, older people) in West Bengal irrespective of their religion will be covered under this scheme. This scheme is applicable to all hospitals (including the private ones) covering all diseases including Covid-19. The treatment provided in the hospital will be entirely cashless under this scheme (Rs. 5 lakh per annum per family to cover the basic health). In Bangladesh, the 'National Policy on Older Person 2013' declared that in every public medical hospital there will be a separate geriatric department. For the female elderly there will be a separate unit and they will be given first priority during service. However, it was found that most of the old age home residents do not know about this scheme and are not being made aware of this scheme. But this policy is essential for their survival during the twilight years of their life.

While summing up this segment we can conclude that the correlates that positively pertain to problems of the elderly at old age homes are financial crisis, health-related problems, lack of family support system, lack of proper medical service, lack of specialized treatment and government schemes.

Suggestions

Ageing being inevitable in human life it is only natural that several physical and mental problems should accompany the process of ageing. However, worries and fears about these problems will merely hasten the decline in physical and mental health. To deal with these problems and ameliorate the plight of the elderly OAH residents in India and Bangladesh, the following steps may be considered.

1. Introducing specialized medical care services

Because of ageing old persons are more likely to fall ill, this calls for emergency treatment. But an inadequate healthcare system poses a serious challenge to the (India and Bangladesh) old age home residents have to go without any specialized treatment. In fact, this is the most intractable problem confronting the old age home residents. What is needed for their survival and physical well-being is a proper medical infrastructure. And the old age home authorities (in both the countries) should make available to them the benefit of specialized medical treatment. An emergency health-funding arrangement should be made to help the elderly old age home residents most of whom are either ultra-poor or below poverty level. Also most of the homes for the aged are lacking Oxygen cylinder facility. Hence, the old age home authorities in India and Bangladesh should arrange for emergency health funding and oxygen cylinder facility. Since most of the old age home residents are not covered by any health insurance policy, the issue of old age homes having an emergency health funding system (for providing treatment to the residents) has become especially important.

2. Introducing the separate sick room

In both India and Bangladesh, there is no arrangement for any separate sick room in almost all the old age homes. The separate sick room is very necessary for the residents' well-being. The old age home authorities in both India and Bangladesh should arrange for such sick rooms to prevent the separate of diseases among the residents.

3. To introduce geriatric hospital and medical care services for the elderly

In order to cater effectively to the special needs of the elderly residents, the homes for the aged (in India and Bangladesh) must provide adequate facilities for diagnosing and treating their diseases and for carrying out tests relating to various geriatric disorders. The old age homes must also have a separate medical-cum-diagnostic unit.

4. Introducing Better Institutional care

The quality of institutional care services available in the old age homes is not up to the mark and more professional health care giving services must be introduced. Also, a proper health check-up system must be developed and a suitable diet should be arranged according to the residents' state of health and special needs. Providing the family environment is also of crucial importance for their mental health. Hence, counselling arrangements should also be made in every old age home to deal with the resident's psychological problems. Care should be taken to heal the psychological and mental wounds of the old age home residents and help erase unpleasant memories. In this regard, the family, the NGOs and the general public should act in close co-ordination to apply the healing touch to the hapless elderly. This should go a long way towards reviving their drooping spirits, and boosting their morale.

5. Facilities in respect of meals

A proper diet schedule is very important for the old age home residents because most of the homes for the elderly in India and Bangladesh do not serve meals according to the residents, state of health and needs. These homes for the aged in both the countries should follow the food chart prescribed by dieticians which would benefit the residents.

6. Introducing an adequate government health scheme

The most worrisome factor for the ageing population is the lack of a proper government policy for the elderly. This is one area where the government must take some specific steps to put in place a medical support system for the poor residents so as to ensure reasonable healthcare in the final phase of their life. The elderly also should be made properly aware of the government medical schemes both in India and Bangladesh. The first and foremost demand of the aged residents is proper medical care. So, the idea is to enable the elderly to access health service easily. The government should provide free-of-cost medical treatment at every hospital, and clinic for the elderly and also take steps to establish a separate geriatric ward in every hospital where the elderly can receive proper treatment. The amount of old age allowance should be enhanced in both the countries. And there is a crying need for a universal health insurance for all the aged persons who live in not only old age homes but also other habitations. Just like the health scheme, the issue of Bank account is also very important. As most of the residents do not have any bank account, they are rendered ineligible for government schemes like old age allowance, widow pension etc. Needless to say, it is very, necessary for their survival. Therefore, the NGOs and old age home authorities should take proper initiatives to enable the poor elderly residents to avail themselves of the bank account facility and the various government schemes. This is applicable to the old age home residents of both the countries. However, it is heartening to note that the government of Bangladesh launched the 'Bayaska Bhata' scheme in 2013 and this scheme will benefit only those elderly who satisfy the eligibility criteria for it they have to be Bangladesh citizen, they have to be disabled to do any work. Those who are widowed or divorced or have no child will get first priority. In this case, the age of the male and the female elderly have to 65 and 62 years respectively. The monthly Bayaska Bhata for 2020-2021 is 500 taka (BD). In India the 'Indira Gandhi National Old Age Pension Scheme' was launched in 1995. This scheme is applicable to all Indian elderly citizens above 60 years of age who belong to below poverty line.

The elderly who are between 60 and 79 years get Rs. 200 per month and those who are above 80 years of age get Rs. 500 per month. The OAH residents in both the countries have said that they do not get any benefit of the old age pension allowance scheme. They have opined that being aware of this scheme would have helped them a lot as they are financially very weak. Therefore, the old age home authorities of both the countries should take steps to help these financially bankrupt elderly residents so that they can obtain much needed support from the government.

Effective action on the basis of the aforesaid suggestions could make the life of the elderly a little more endurable and even enjoyable. Admittedly, the problems associated with old age can never be totally eliminated. But steps should undeniably be taken to mitigate them.

REFERENCES

Abedin, S., (2003). "Living and care arrangements of the elderly in Bangladesh". In Kabir, M. (Ed.). *The Elderly—Contemporary Issues* (pp. 100-107). Dhaka: Dhaka Presidency Press.

Bangladesh Bureau of Statistics and Information Division, Ministry of Planning. (2014). Bangladesh Population and Housing Census 2011. Retrieved from www.bbs.gov.bd on 22-07-2019 at 12.00 p.m.

Bardhan, A. (2014). "Impact of Old Age Allowance Program on Older Persons in Bangladesh: A Study". *Bangladesh Journal of Geritrics*, Vol. 49, pp. 217-224.

Bangladesh Bureau of Statistics and Information Division, Ministry of Planning. (2014). Bangladesh Population Census Report 2011. Dhaka: BBS retrieved from www.bbs.gov.bd on 28-07-2019 at 8.30 p.m.

Barikdar, A., Ahmed, T., Lasker, S., (2016). "The Situation of the Elderly in Bangladesh". *Bangladesh Journal of Bioethics*, 7(1): 27-36.

Bhuiyan, I., (1998). "Importance of Health and Welfare Programs for the Elderly in Bangladesh". *Bangladesh Journal of Geriatrics*; Vol. 34, pp. 21-35.

Chakravarty, I., Alam, M., Mazumdar, S., Yadav, P., (2014). *The Status of Elderly in West Bengal*, 2011. Retrieved from http://www.isec.ac.in/West%20Bengal.pdf on 22-07-2019 at 11.30 a.m.

Chen *et al.,* (2014). "Prevalence and Associated Factors of Frailty among Elderly people in Taiwan". *International Journal of Gerontology*, 8(3): 114-119.

Dani, P.. (2018). "A Comparative Study to Assess the Quality of Life Among Senior Citizens Residing at Homes and Old Age Homes of Pune City." Doctoral Dissertation, Bharati Vidyapeeth Deemed University, Pune.

Government of the People's Republic of Bangladesh, (2013). National Policy of Older Person (Jatiya Probin Nitimala 2013). Ministry of Social Welfare, Dhaka, Bangladesh.

Government of India, (2011). *Census of India 2011*. From http://censusindia.gov.in/ . Retrieved on 14-02-2021 at 14:20.

Government of India. (2007). Maintenance and Welfare of Parents and Senior Citizens Act, 2007. 56/2007. Government of India. New Delhi, the Gazette of India.

Government of India, (2015). An Integrated Programme for Older Persons. 2015, retrieved from http://socialjustice.nic.in/ipop.php on 15-01-2021 at 8:25 am

Government of India, (2016). Elderly in India—Profile and Programmes 2016. Central statistics Office Ministry of Statistics and Programme Implementation Government of India retrieved from http://mospi.nic.in/sites/default/files/publicationreports/ElderlyinIndia 2016.pdf on 11-05-2020 at 9.14 p.m.

Isha, M., (2016). "Quality of Life in Old Age Homes in Punjab: A Study of Institutionalized Elderly". *Elk Asia Pacific Journal of Social Sciences*, 2(2): 1-19.

Hurlock, E.B., (2005). *Development Psychology: A Life Span Approach*. Tata McGraw-Hill Publication Company Limited, New Delhi.

Khole, C., Soletti, A., (2018). "Nutritional Status of Elderly in the Old Age Homes: A Study in Pune City". *Journal of Current Research in Nutrition and Food Science*, 6(1), 234-240.

4
Self Help Groups and Livelihood Security among the Elderly Population

Ritwika Rajendra and *Pranita Ghalay*

Introduction

An SHG typically consists of 10 to 20 members who collectively engage in regular savings, lending, and other initiatives. The SHGs have shown to be beneficial in enhancing and expanding existing livelihoods options by offering necessary skill training and by providing cost-effective credit. The inclusion of the elderly into self-help groups has been an initiative of the Government as well as the Non-Governmental Organizations. An Elderly Self Help Group (ESHG) is a group of 10 to 20 elderly aged 55 and above who form a group based on self-selection. The groups are mostly homogeneous with respect to gender. The elderly SHG members are still productive, having moved into supplementary livelihoods from their primary occupations. The process of forming Elderly SHGs begins with a number of meetings with the village elderly to motivate them and to explain the concept. Once the group is formed, each member of the Elderly SHG is motivated to save on a monthly or fortnightly basis. Each group maintains four sets of books/records: a general minutes (and resolution) register, a savings register, a credit register, and individual passbooks. Initially, the saved fund, for which a ledger is maintained, is deposited in the bank in a joint account. The groups are assisted to establish these first linkages with the banks. Accompanying the groups in opening the initial bank account is very important since many elderly have never used banking services in their entire life and are unfamiliar with basic banking formalities. National Rural Livelihood Mission supports structures that have been set up at the national, state, district, and sub-district levels which facilitate the elderly with the government benefits for better functioning as a Self Help Group member. According to a study conducted in Bihar 2015, ESHGs not only provide an economic opportunity but also strengthen the capacities of the elderly to save and create a spirit of entrepreneurship. They can promote empowerment of the elderly by supporting collective action and advocacy for their rights and entitlements, thereby acting as an important peer group beyond the network of family, friends, and neighbours. Furthermore, strong grassroots level ESHGs and their federations can provide social assistance to fellow destitute elders.

NABARD being the principal agent in rural development in India has defined the concept of SHGs as small, economically homogeneous affinity groups of rural poor, voluntarily formed to save and mutually contribute to a common fund to be lent to its members as per the group members' decision. Of course, when it was initially given, its objective was to carry on saving and lending activities among its members to promote and enhance their economic and social standards. Micro-finance seeks to cover the socio-economic condition and educational attainment of the member's family, their supporting system, availability of funds and loans, training facilities, and marketing process of products. SHG is a group rather it is a well-managed group where members evolve some rules and regulations on which are to be adopted, after discussion with all the members. It is a voluntary homogenous group of 10-20 individuals from weaker sections (particularly women) engaged in agriculture, small business in rural areas. Member having common interest among each other things and member save regularly and contribute to a common fund. The members agree to use this common fund and other funds like grants and loans from banks, which they may receive as a group, to give small loans to needy members as per the decision of the group. In Self Help Group, members mobilize the resources of the individual member for their collective economic development and uplift the living condition of poor as hence the member create a habit of savings and utilization of local resources. SHG identifies the problems, analyse and finds a solution in the group, assists the member financially at the time of need. In simple words, it acts as a medium for socio-economic development. In India, though SHGs are formed for various purposes, the main objectives behind SHGs are – promotion of livelihoods of their members through collective savings and investment activities which make them self-reliant and self-sufficient. The concept of and the idea behind SHGs is of recent origin. They not only play a major role in poverty alleviation in rural India but are instrumental in creating consciousness among a section of persons who are otherwise ignored and neglected people below the poverty line, mostly women voluntarily joining SHGs as a member. In recent times both the member and their membership is constantly increasing all over India. They not only engage themselves in solving and investment activities which are commonly believed to be the functions of the SHGs but also in some other more socially and economically desirable activities like income generation, environmental conservation, literacy, child care, and nutrition. The SHG system is designed to be effective in empowering rural women below the poverty line. Economic and social empowerment is one of the basic components of SHGs development.

Concept of Self Help Groups

The origin of Self Help Groups (SHGs) is the brainchild of Grameen Bank of Bangladesh, founded by Prof. Mohammed Yunus in 1975, who tried out a new approach to rural credit in Bangladesh. In India, NABARD initiated SHGs in the year 1986-87 but the real effort was taken after 1991-92 from the linkage of SHGs with the banks. SHGs play a major role in rural India as it is the instrument for women empowerment. Through SHG women are capable of taking decisions and are economically and socially empowered. It is a boon for the rural poor. SHG is a small group of rural poor, who have voluntarily come forward to form a group for improvement of the social and economic status of the members. It can be formal (registered) or informal. The concept underlines the principle of thrift, credit, and Self Help. Members of SHG agree to save regularly and contribute to a common fund and use this common fund and such other funds (like grants and loans from banks), which they may receive as a group, to give small loans to needy members as per the decision of the group. The SHG provides not only a savings mechanism, which suits the needs of the members but also provides a cost-effective delivery mechanism for a small credit to its members.

Self Help Groups and Elderly

Elderly women are incapacitated due to various reasons as most of them are socially backward, have health issues, are illiterate, and poor economic base. Individually an elderly woman is not only weak in the socio-economic term but also lacks access to knowledge and information. However, in a group, they are empowered to overcome many of these weaknesses. Hence, there are needs for SHGs. NABARD being the principal agent in rural development in India has defined the concept of SHGs as small, economically homogeneous affinity groups of rural poor, voluntarily formed to save and mutually contribute to a common fund to be lent to its members as per the group member's decision. The concept of and the idea behind SHGs is of recent origin. They not only play a major role in poverty alleviation in rural India but are instrumental in creating consciousness among a section of persons who are otherwise ignored and neglected people and below the poverty line mostly women. In recent times both the member and their membership is constantly increasing all over India. They not only engage themselves in solving and investment activities which are commonly believed to be the functions of the SHGs but also in some other more socially and economically desirable activities like income generation, environmental conservation, literacy, child care, and nutrition. The SHG system is designed to be effective in empowering rural women below the poverty line. Economic and social empowerment is one of the basic components of SHGs development. The emergence and rapid multiplication of Self Help Groups (SHGs) based on microcredit is a phenomenon that is gaining increasing importance in the development scenario. Today there are seven million SHGs in the country. Nearly 90 per cent of the groups are women groups.

Self Help Groups and livelihood security of elderly

Women are an integral part of every society. We can't think about a society without women. So the place of women in society is one of the fundamental aspects of any civilization, ancient or modern because the relationship between men and women is so vital that it affects almost every aspect of man's society. Generally, it is believed that women are mothers, wives, sisters, and daughters. They have to cook, do all households works, take care of men, and are subordinate to male authority. But when they become old, their family members neglect them and keep them aside. Their health gets deteriorated, their physical problems and economic problems arise. They are largely excluded from high-status occupation and power position of power. And they keep themselves as an active member of Self Help Groups. In the SHGs, they earn their livelihood through different kinds of income generation activities. The main objectives of SHGs are the promotion of livelihood of their members through savings and interest at the concept of SHG is that-it is a voluntary homogeneous group of 10 to 20 individuals from weaker sections, particularly women, engaged in various types of activities with the help of their saving money and member also agree to use this purpose, i.e., saving money. Whenever the member of a particular group requires money, the group gives small loans to needy members as per the decision made by the group.

Conclusion

The elderly have become a target of all developmental activities all over the country, whether it is rehabilitation or livelihood security. SHGs are an effective way to secure the livelihood of the elderly population, especially in rural areas. Since SHGs provide a base for the elderly populations to work together in groups for undertaking economic activities that will help them to have an alternative source of income. Individuals who are a part of SHGs have a greater possibility of being economically independent. Members of a Self-Help Group can mobilise resources for their collective economic growth which helps improve the living conditions of the elderly. The SHG model is aimed at enabling rural women living below the poverty line to achieve economic empowerment. SHGs through its economic activities can be a way of achieving a dignified life for the elderly who are otherwise underserved. One of the core elements of SHGs is economic growth and social empowerment.

In terms of social development, SHGs also play a crucial role in providing the group members social and emotional support. Since the members of an SHG are usually from the same geographical location, they know the dynamics of each household. Thus, through a group individuals can seek support if they are facing issues in the family or community. At an individual level too, SHG members are able to provide support to one another. Thus, SHGs are important for the economic independence of the elderly populations as the social support of the group members.

REFERENCES

Alam, M., & Yadav, P., (2015). Enhancing Livelihood Opportunities for the Elderly: A Qualitative Study of Elderly Self-Self Groups from two Districts of Tamil Nadu, (January 2016). Retrieved from https://www.researchgate.net/publication/290439509

Deutsche Gesellschaft für Internationale Zusammenarbeit (GIZ) (2015). Impact of Elderly Self-Help Groups on Quality of Life of Elders in Bihar: Assessment of Community Managed Grassroots Institutions Promoting Old Age Protection.

NRLM Handbook on Social Inclusion, Available at: http://nirdpr.org.in/nird_docs/nrlm/nrlmhandbookSocialInclusion050716.pdf

Sahar, J., Riasmini, N.M., Kusumawati, D.N., & Erawati, E., (2017). "Improved Health Status and Life Satisfaction among Older People following Self-Help Group Intervention in Jakarta". *Current Gerontology and Geriatrics Research* https://doi.org/10.1155/2017/387906

5

Role of Panchayat for Implementation of Indira Gandhi National Old Age Pension Scheme

A Case Study of Katigorah GP, Cachar, Assam

Md Abdul Ahad Borbhuiya and *Azmal Hussain*

Introduction

The Department of Social Welfare has been assigned the responsibility of mitigating the traditional exploitation of the poor and unprivileged sections of the society, besides bridging the social gaps among various strata of population. For the achievement of this objective, various benefit oriented schemes have been launched from time to time to bring unprivileged and underprivileged within the ambit of schemes so as to transform them into useful citizens of the society and facilitate their life with dignity and social honour. The Indira Gandhi National Old Age Pension Scheme (IGNOAPS) is a social sector scheme and forms part of the National Social Assistance Programme (NSAP) which came into effect from 15th August, 1995.

This IGNOAPS scheme is meant for the old age people who are above 60 years of age (revised later from 65 years) and who live below the poverty line. Through this scheme, a monthly cash is provided to these old age people which is currently Rs. 200 per month for person aged in 60–79 range. For applicants aged above 80 years, the amount Rs. 500 a month, that is revised in 2011. State government can also add their part in it, which they usually do.

Objectives of IGNOAPS

The main objective behind the scheme was to fulfil the spirit of Article 41 which comes under directive principle of state policy.

Article 41 says:

> "Right to work, to education and to public assistance in certain cases The State shall, within the limits of its economic capacity and development, make effective provision for securing the right to work, to education and to public assistance in cases of unemployment, old age, sickness and disablement, and in other cases of undeserved want."

The programme formulated a National Policy for Social Assistance for the poor and aims at ensuring minimum national standard for social assistance. These new assistance are addition to the benefits that states are currently providing or might provide in future

Eligibility and Scope: The eligibility criteria of the scheme is as under:—

I. The age of destitute (male or female) should be 65 years or above. As per the revised eligibility criteria the age has been reduced to 60 years instead of 65 years w.e.f. 1st April, 2011.
II. He/she must be destitute in the sense of having little or no regular source of subsistence/financial supports from other family members or other sources.
III. He/she must belong to a household living below the poverty line according to the criteria prescribed by the Govt. of India.
IV. The central contribution of pension under the scheme is Rs. 200/ per month per beneficiary and the state Govt. can contribute over and above to this amount out of State resources. At present, every beneficiary is getting Rs. 400 per month with a break-up of Rs. 200 each from Central and State share. In the revised guidelines the Central share would remain unchanged in respect of beneficiaries in the age group of 60-79 years. However, it would be enhanced to Rs. 500 per month per beneficiary aged 80 years and above w.e.f. 1st April, 2011.

Procedure

a. The eligible persons are required to apply on an application form devised for the purpose and available in the Social Welfare Department.
b. Voter identity card is required as age proof of the applicant.
c. The income and destitute criteria is determined on the certificate issued by a Gazetted Officer and Revenue authorities of the area to which the applicant belongs.

d. The applicant must have BPL card or his/her name must be registered in the BPL register maintained for the purpose.

e. The applications are furnished to the concerned Tehsil Social Welfare officers where these are thoroughly scrutinized/verified and the list of bona fide cases is recommended to the District Social Welfare Officer. The final sanction is accorded by District Level Sanctioning Committee (DLSC) constituted for the purpose under the Chairmanship of District Development Commissioner concerned.

Mode of Payment: The payment is disbursed to the beneficiaries through payee's bank account on monthly/Quarterly basis at Katigorah GP after properly checking their identity cards issued to them for receipt of the pension under IGNOAPS.

Objectives of the Study: The study was planned to be conceived with the following objectives:—

I. To assess the progress *vis-à-vis* targets both Physical and Financial of the Scheme.

II. To assess ground realities with regard to coverage, identification procedure, selection and sanctioning of cases.

III. To assess the impact of the scheme on Targeted beneficiaries.

Research Methodology

The article on "Role of Panchayat for Implementing Indira Gandhi National Old Age Pension Schemre: A Case Study of Katigorah GP, Cachar, Assam" has been conducted by using primary data and secondary data. Primary data has been collected through well-devised schedule. Besides, secondary information has also been collected from various sources, viz., books, journals, websites, newspapers etc. In this research paper, three parameters such as financial inputs, beneficiary profile, and beneficiary status are considered. It is based on convenience sampling. The data collected has been tabulated, analyzed and interpreted for drawing conclusions. After the analysis of the data, few suggestions are made at the end.

Financial Input: Under Indira Gandhi National Old Age Pension Scheme (IGNOAPS), a sum of Rs. 400 per month is provided at Katigorah GP for registered beneficiaries through the Social Welfare Department. The Input of the Scheme is basically the financial allocation earmarked for it and, of course, the efforts of the Social Welfare Department in identifying the deserving persons, processing their cases and finally disbursing the amount envisaged under it. The Evaluation Process is the input and output analysis of the Scheme and naturally before analyzing the outputs in terms of realization of stipulated objectives, the assessment of inputs of the scheme has to be made. The instant study has been confined to Katigorah GP and the reference period stands restricted to the years 2014-15 to 2016-17. Table 5.1 provides information on the financial inputs required, provided and actually disbursed to the beneficiaries during the reference period.

Table 5.1

(Figures in rupees)

Sl. No.	Year	Amount required	Amount provided	% of amount provided	% of amount utilized
1	2014-15	69000	41600	60.28%	100%
2	2015-16	81000	49400	60.99%	100%
3	2016-17	89200	56000	62.78%	100%

Details of Allocation and Expenditure 2014-15 to 2016-17.
Source: Katigorah GP office.

Well the percentage of amount utilisation is 100 per cent in every year, but early year there was a scam made by office authorities because of cash in hand transaction, but now it is not possible because of e-transaction payment method. In fact, the scheme modalities require the Social Welfare Department to continue the process of identification, processing and sanctioning of cases under IGNOAPS together with the process of weeding-out non-deserving/uneligible cases, mainly occurring due to deaths. On the basis of net number of beneficiaries, the Department of Social Welfare Projects the demand before the government for the next financial year. As per the modalities of the Govt. of India governing the IGNOAPS, the states have been provided estimated number of beneficiaries and they are required to identify all the eligible beneficiaries up to that estimate for obtaining central assistance. In case the coverage exceeds the estimated limit, the expenditure on excess number of beneficiaries has to be borne by the respective state governments from their own funds

It also needs special mention here that schemes with high fund utilization efficiency are equally vulnerable to misappropriation, particularly, when proper supervisory and monitoring system fails to perform in an effective manner.

Beneficiary Profile: The number of beneficiaries who were covered in the Katigorah GP under IGNOAPS for disbursement of pension is provided in Table 5.2 along with ancillary information.

Table 5.2

(Unit in No's)

Sl.No	Years	60-79	80 to above	Total
1	2014-15	182	13	195
2	2015-16	213	17	230
3	2016-17	240	20	260

Details of beneficiary coverage under IGNOAPS.
Source: Katigorah GP office.

The launching of social assistance schemes like the IGNOAPS is under constitutional obligation of the Govt. to provide public assistance to its citizens in case of old age, sickness, disablement etc. within the limit of its resources. All citizens being equal, these schemes require to be demand.

Here the data is combined of both male and female. The number of beneficiary is gradually increasing year by year but the amount which have been provided by the government not increasing respectively. On the other hand so far as inflation concerned today's money is not equal to tomorrow's money so the quantum of money should be increased.

Field Findings: The ground position of IGNOAPS beneficiaries was of mixed nature which is reflected in table 5.3.

Table 5.3

(Unit in No's)

Sl. No.	Description	60-79			80 to above		
		2014-15	2015-16	2016-17	2014-15	2015-16	2016-17
1	Eligible beneficiary for IGNOAPS	299	347	380	23	29	33
2	Beneficiary actually found and contacted	182	213	240	13	17	20
3	Eligible but not getting	117	134	140	10	12	13

Ground Position of IGNOAPS beneficiaries.
Source: Katigorah GP office.

Across the Katigorah GP, there are 413 eligible beneficiaries for IGNOAPS, but only 260 are receiving assistance under IGNOAPS as on 31-3-2017. In one side all eligible candidates are not getting the benefit of IGNOAPS and on the other side, the ratio between getting and not getting the benefit of IGNPAPS is not reducing rather it is increasing day by day. Eligible, but not getting the benefits only because of biasness of the selection team. The members of the selection team always focus on their relatives and neighbours. Most of the people are died in between 70 to 79 years so the number of beneficiary in 80 to above is less as compared to 60 to 79 years old beneficiary. If a person dies then it is replaced by others who are eligible.

Impact of IGNOAPS at Katigorah: The impacts of Indira Gandhi National Old Age Pension Scheme on the beneficiaries of Katigorah GP are as follows:

- They feel financial security.
- They do not depend on others.
- Sometimes they can able to help others by providing credit facility.
- Their living status also increased.
- They can take care of them self and also other family members too.

Suggestions

There have suggestions which are made after analysing and interpreting the data collected from Katigorah GP office and also from ground field of Katigorah GP. These suggestions are:

- Selection process should be unbiased.
- Selection committee should not have any political person.
- Amount should be given to all eligible persons.
- Selection committee should update the beneficiary list regularly.

Conclusion

From the above discussion we have find that IGNOAPS is good but it is not given to all eligible candidate. The candidates who are enjoying this benefit they feel little bit secure in the context of finance. Because of political benefit, the selection committee always focus on politically useful candidates. Some candidates also getting benefit on their merit list.

Moreover, the amount which is required at Katigorah GP, the same amount is not provided by the government.

REFERENCES

http://ecostatjk.nic.in/ecosurvey/Evaluation%20Report%20on%20%20IGNOAPS.pdf

http://www.simplydecoded.com/2013/01/12/national-social-assistance-programme-introduction/

https://www.ncbi.nlm.nih.gov/pmc/.../PMC50719

www.ideasforindia.in/article.aspx?article_id=336

Section-II:
Old age Issues, Limitations and Problems

6
Health issues of Older Persons

Dipak Sarkar

Introduction

Old age is a mutual disengagement between people and their society occurs in anticipation of death by becoming a disengaged from work and family responsibilities. According to this concept, people are enabling to enjoy their old age without stress. The changing demographic scenario and population projections of India indicate that the growth rate of Indian older adults is comparatively faster than other regions of the world. In India, Health issues are common in old age but frequently remain undetected and untreated. Some of the common health issues of older persons in our country include functional disability, disturb rehabilitation, burden the health system and impair life-quality of old-patients and their relatives. Health is the basis of remaining autonomy and life quality in old age. Besides curing a patient, assurement of life-quality of the multi-morbid old patients should be the main goal of medical gerontology. Not only internal medicine, but also great arrays of medical disciplines will have to cooperate to reach this objective.

Risk factors of ill health among older people: As people age, they become more susceptible to disease and disability. However, much of the burden of ill health among older people can be reduced or prevented by adequately addressing specific risk factors, including—

- **Injury:** Falls and the injuries to which they often lead cause a large share of the burden of disease and disability on older people. The risk of falls increases steeply with age. Injuries from falls usually require hospitalization and costly interventions, including rehabilitation, and cause much of the functional limitations that lead to the need for long-term care, including admissions to nursing homes.

- **Non-communicable diseases:** Healthy ageing is a lifelong process. Patterns of harmful behaviour, often established early in life, can reduce the quality of life and even result in premature death. Poor nutrition, physical inactivity, tobacco use and harmful use of alcohol contribute to the development of chronic conditions.
- **Poverty:** The risk of poverty grows with older age and is much higher among women than men. Many older people cannot afford to pay health costs, including prescription drugs, from their own pockets.
- **Social isolation and exclusion, mental health disorders:** Loneliness, social isolation and social exclusion are important social determinants and risk factors of ill health among older people. They affect all aspects of health and well-being, including mental health, the risk of maltreatment and the risk of emergency admission to hospital for avoidable conditions, such as severe dehydration or malnutrition.
- **Elder maltreatment:** Elder maltreatment is defined as physical, sexual, mental and/or financial abuse and/or neglect of people aged 60 years and older. Maltreatment affects both the mental and physical well-being of older people and, if unchecked, reduces the quality of life and survival.

Health issue of older person

1. **Chronic health conditions:** According to the National Council on Aging, about 92 per cent of seniors have at least one chronic disease and 77 per cent have at least two. Heart disease, stroke, cancer, and diabetes are among the most common and costly chronic health conditions causing two-thirds of deaths each year. The National Center for Chronic Disease Prevention and Health Promotion recommends meeting with a physician for an annual check-up, maintaining a healthy diet and keeping an exercise routine to help manage or prevent chronic diseases. Obesity is a growing problem among older adults and engaging in these lifestyle behaviours can help reduce obesity and associated chronic conditions.
2. **Cognitive health:** Cognitive health is focused on a person's ability to think, learn and remember. The most common cognitive health issue facing the elderly is dementia, the loss of those cognitive

functions. Approximately 47.5 million people worldwide have dementia, a number that is predicted to nearly triple in size by 2050. The most common form of dementia is Alzheimer's disease with as many as five million people over the age of 65 suffering from the disease in the United States. According to the National Institute on Aging, other chronic health conditions and diseases increase the risk of developing dementia, such as substance abuse, diabetes, hypertension, depression, HIV and smoking. While there are no cures for dementia, physicians can prescribe a treatment plan and medications to manage the disease.

3. **Mental health:** According to the World Health Organization, over 15 per cent of adults over the age of 60 suffer from a mental disorder. A common mental disorder among seniors is depression, occurring in seven per cent of the elderly population. Unfortunately, this mental disorder is often underdiagnosed and undertreated. Older adults account for over 18 per cent of suicides deaths in the United States. Because depression can be a side effect of chronic health conditions, managing those conditions help. Additionally, promoting a lifestyle of healthy living such as betterment of living conditions and social support from family, friends or support groups can help treat depression.
4. **Physical injury:** Every 15 seconds, an older adult is admitted to the emergency room for a fall. A senior dies from falling every 29 minutes, making it the leading cause of injury among the elderly. Because aging causes bones to shrink and muscle to lose strength and flexibility, seniors are more susceptible to losing their balance, bruising and fracturing a bone. Two diseases that contribute to frailty are osteoporosis and osteoarthritis. However, falls are not inevitable. In many cases, they can be prevented through education, increased physical activity and practical modifications within the home.
5. **HIV/AIDS and other sexually transmitted diseases:** In 2013, the Center for Disease Control and Prevention (CDC) found that 21 per cent of AIDS cases occurred in seniors over the age of 50 in the United States, and 37 per cent of deaths that same year were people over the age of 55. While sexual needs and ability may change as people age, sexual desire doesn't disappear completely. Seniors are unlikely to use condoms, which, when combined with a weakened immune system, makes the elderly more susceptible to contracting HIV. Late diagnosis of HIV is common among older adults because symptoms of HIV are very similar to those of

normal aging, making it more difficult to treat and prevent damage to the immune system.

6. **Malnutrition:** Malnutrition in older adults over the age of 65 is often underdiagnosed and can lead to other elderly health issues, such as a weakened immune system and muscle weakness. The causes of malnutrition can stem from other health problems (seniors suffering from dementia may forget to eat), depression, alcoholism, dietary restrictions, reduced social contact and limited income. Committing to small changes in diet, such as increasing consumption of fruits and vegetables and decreasing consumption of saturated fat and salt, can help nutrition issues in the elderly. There are food services available to older adults who cannot afford food or have difficulty in preparing meals.
7. **Sensory impairments:** Sensory impairments, such as vision and hearing, are extremely common for older Americans over the age of 70. According to the CDC, one out of six older adults has a visual impairment and one out of four has a hearing impairment. Luckily, both of these issues are easily treatable by aids such as glasses or hearing aids. New technologies are enhancing assessment of hearing loss and wear ability of hearing aids.
8. **Oral health:** Often overlooked, oral health is one of the most important issues for the elderly. The CDC's Division of Oral Health found that about 25 per cent of adults over the age of 65 no longer have their natural teeth. Problems such as cavities and tooth decay can lead to difficulty maintaining a healthy diet, low self-esteem, and other health conditions. Oral health issues associated with older adults are dry mouth, gum disease and mouth cancer. These conditions could be managed or prevented by making regular dental check-ups. Dental care, however, can be difficult for seniors to access due to loss of dental insurance after retirement or economical disadvantages.
9. **Substance abuse:** Substance abuse, typically alcohol or drug-related, is more prevalent among seniors than realized. According to the National Council on Aging, the number of older adults with substance abuse problems is expected to double to five million by 2020. Additionally, older adults are often prescribed multiple prescriptions to be used long-term. The National Institute on Drugs finds that substance abuse typically results from someone suffering mental deficits or taking another patient's medication due to their inability to pay for their own.

10. **Bladder control and constipation:** Incontinence and constipation are both common with aging, and can impact older adults quality of life. In addition to age-related changes, these may be a side effect of previous issues mentioned above, such as not eating a well-balanced diet and suffering from chronic health conditions. The Mayo Clinic suggests maintaining a healthy weight, eating a healthy diet and exercising regularly to avoid these elderly health issues. There are often effective medical treatments, and older adults should not be embarrassed to discuss with their physicians.

Remedial measures

1. **Health care and nutrition:** Health care needs of older persons must be given high priority, the primary health care system will be strengthened and oriented to meet the health care needs of older persons.
2. **Shelter:** Housing schemes for urban and rural lower income segments should earmark 10 per cent of the houses/house sites for allotment to Older persons older persons will be given easy access to loans for purchase of housing and for major repairs with easy repayment schedules. A multi-purpose center for older persons is a necessity for social interaction and it will be necessary to earmark sites for such centers in all housing colonies. Preferences will be given to older persons in the allotment of flats on the ground floor.
3. **Education:** Discrimination against older persons for availing opportunities for education, training and orientation should be removed. Assistance for open universities will be sought to develop packages using distance learning techniques. Educational curriculum at all stages of formal education as also non-formal education programmes should incorporate material to strengthen intergenerational bonds and mutually supporting relationships.
4. **Law:** The introduction of special provisions in IPC to protect older persons from domestic violence must be considered and machinery provided to attend to all such cases promptly. Tenancy legislation need to be reviewed so that the rights of occupancy of older persons are restored speedily.
5. **Media:** The policy aims to involve mass media on ageing issues to provide opportunities to media personnel to have access to

information. Apart from their own independent sources their participation in orientation programmes on ageing will be facilitated.

6. **Income security in old age:** A major intervention required in old age relates to financial insecurity as more than two third of the elderly live below the poverty line. It would increase with age uniformly across the country.
7. **Indira Gandhi National Old Age Pension Scheme:** Old age pension scheme should cover all senior citizens living below the poverty line. Rate of monthly pension should be raised to Rs. 1000 per month per person and revised at intervals to prevent its deflation due to higher cost of purchasing.
8. **Public distribution system:** The public distribution system must reach out to cover all senior citizens living below the poverty line.
9. **Establishment of national council for senior citizens:** A national council for senior citizens, headed by the minister for social justice and empowerment should be constituted by the Ministry. The council should include representatives of relevant central ministries, the Planning Commission and ten states by rotation. Representative of NGOs, academia, media and expert on ageing.
10. **Provide equal access:** Provide equal access to food, shelter, medical and other services to senior citizens during and after natural disasters and emergencies.

Conclusion

Effective treatment of the older people suffering from mental and other problems requires a comprehensive use of medical, psychological, sociological procedure. The treatment has to be administered depending upon the needs of the individuals. Some requires just dietary measures while some other may need a surgical operation. Many report have revealed that both individual and group psychotherapy would yield favourable results in treating mental disorder associated with old age. Administration of group therapy or socio therapy to older patient would mean the creating of a social environment in which the person can function successfully. It should also include working with the family in an attempt to help them understand the nature of the patient's disorder, to be supportive, and to show that they care.

REFERENCES

Developing Mental Health and Coping Skills, Dept. of Educational Psychology and Foundation of Education, NCERT, 2009.

http://www.euro.who.int/en/health-topics/Life-stages/healthy-ageing/data-and-statistics/risk-factors-of-ill-health-among-older-people

Shankar Rao, C.N., *Sociology Principle of Sociology with an Introduction to Social Thought.*

7

Mental Disorders among Older Adults

Identifying Risk Factors and Remedial Measures

Surajit Kar

Introduction

Older adults, those aged 60 or above, make important contribution to society as family members, volunteers and as active participants in the workforce. While most have good mental health, many older adults are at risk of developing mental disorders, neurological disorders or substance use problems. Older adults are also vulnerable to elder abuse – including physical, verbal, psychological, financial and sexual abuse; abandonment; neglect; and serious losses of dignity and respect. Current evidence suggests that 1 in 10 older people experience elder abuse. Elder abuse can lead not only to physical injuries, but also to serious, sometimes long lasting psychological consequences, including depression and anxiety. Older people may experience life stressors common to all people, but also stressors that are more common in later life, like a significant ongoing loss in capacities and a decline in functional ability. In addition, older people are more likely to experience events such as bereavement, or a drop in socio-economic status with retirement. All of these stressors can result in isolation, loneliness or psychological distress in older people, for which they may require long-term care.

Risk factors for mental health problems among older adults

There may be multiple risk factors for mental health problems at any point in life. Older people may experience life stressors common to all people, but also stressors that are more common in later life, like a significant ongoing loss in capacities and a decline in functional ability. For example, older adults may experience reduced mobility, chronic pain, frailty or other health problems, for which they require some form of long-term care. In addition, older people are more likely to experience events such as bereavement, or a drop in socio-economic status with retirement. All of these stressors can result in isolation, loneliness or psychological distress in older people, for which they may require long-term care.

Mental health has an impact on physical health and *vice versa*. For example, older adults with physical health conditions such as heart disease have higher rates of depression than those who are healthy. Additionally, untreated depression in an older person with heart disease can negatively affect its outcome.

Dementia and depression among older people as public health issues

Dementia

Dementia is a syndrome, usually of a chronic or progressive nature, in which there is deterioration in memory, thinking, behaviour and the ability to perform everyday activities. It mainly affects older people, although it is not a normal part of ageing. There are significant social and economic issues in terms of the direct costs of medical, social and informal care associated with dementia. Moreover, physical, emotional and economic pressures can cause great stress to families and careers. Support is needed from the health, social, financial and legal systems for both people with dementia and their careers.

Depression

Depression is the most common mental disorder in older people. However, symptoms can be distinctly different to depression in young adults, and it is often missed. The risk factors for depression include physical health problems, female gender, loneliness, life events (particularly bereavement) and loss of independence. Older adults can present with the same symptoms as younger adults: Core symptoms (low mood, reduced enjoyment, lack of energy), psychological symptoms (low self-esteem, hopelessness/guilt, suicidal thoughts), and biological symptoms (reduced appetite, weight loss, feeling lower in morning, early wakening, reduced sleep, poor concentration, agitation or slowness). Certain symptoms are more common in older adults and might be the only presenting features:

1. Reporting physical rather than emotional symptoms (somatization). Typical symptoms are: faintness or dizziness, pain, weakness all over, heavy limbs, lump in throat, constipation.

2. Health anxieties (hypochondriasis), especially if unusual for the person.
3. Prominent anxiety.
4. Unusual behaviour. Hysteria does not exist in older people.
5. Slowing-down of emotional reactions or agitation.
6. Psychotic features (delusions of guilt, poverty or physical illness, or having no clothes which fit. Auditory hallucinations with derogatory or obscene content, provoking guilt and paranoia).

A sensitive indicator for the diagnosis of depression includes lacking interest in something previously enjoyed. A measure of the severity of that depression is to ask if people enjoy visits from their grandchildren. People, who don't, tend to be very depressed. Mood congruent delusions are present in psychotic depression. These are delusions reflecting the person's low mood—such as ideas of poverty, having no clothes which fit, of impending death, or Cotard's syndrome (where a person feels that their insides are dead). Ask if people deserve the content of their delusions. If they say yes, they might well be depressed. Sometimes, the presentation of depression can be atypical, many people will be familiar with what we used to call amitriptyline deficiency syndrome (sertraline deficiency syndrome would be the obvious modern equivalent).

Treatment and care strategies to address mental health needs of older people: It is important to prepare health providers and societies to meet the specific needs of older populations, including:

- training for health professionals in providing care for older people;
- preventing and managing age-associated chronic diseases including mental, neurological and substance use disorders;
- designing sustainable policies on long-term and palliative care; and
- developing age-friendly services and settings.

Health promotion: The mental health of older adults can be improved through promoting Active and Healthy Ageing. Mental health-specific health promotion for older adults involves creating living conditions and environments that support well-being and allow people to lead a healthy life. Promoting mental health depends largely on strategies to ensure that older people have the necessary resources to meet their needs, such as:

- providing security and freedom;
- adequate housing through supportive housing policy;
- social support for older people and their caregivers;

- health and social programmes targeted at vulnerable groups such as those who live alone and rural populations or who suffer from a chronic or relapsing mental or physical illness;
- programmes to prevent and deal with elder abuse; and
- community development programmes.

Interventions: Prompt recognition and treatment of mental, neurological and substance use disorders in older adults is essential. Both psychosocial interventions and medicines are recommended. There is no medication currently available to cure dementia but much can be done to support and improve the lives of people with dementia and their caregivers and families, such as:

- early diagnosis, in order to promote early and optimal management;
- optimizing physical and mental health, functional ability and well-being;
- identifying and treating accompanying physical illness;
- detecting and managing challenging behaviour; and
- providing information and long-term support to careers.

Mental health care in the community: Good general health and social care is important for promoting older people's health, preventing disease and managing chronic illnesses. Training all health providers in working with issues and disorders related to ageing is therefore important. Effective, community-level primary mental health care for older people is crucial. It is equally important to focus on the long-term care of older adults suffering from mental disorders, as well as to provide caregivers with education, training and support. An appropriate and supportive legislative environment based on internationally accepted human rights standards is required to ensure the highest quality of services to people with mental illness and their caregivers.

WHO response: WHO supports governments in the goal of strengthening and promoting mental health in older adults and to integrate effective strategies into policies and plans. The global strategy and action plan on ageing and health was adopted by the World Health Assembly in 2016. One of the objectives of this global strategy is to align the health systems to the needs of older populations, for mental as well as physical health. Key actions include: orienting health systems around intrinsic capacity and functional ability, developing and ensuring affordable access to quality older person-centered and integrated clinical care, and ensuring a sustainable and appropriately trained, deployed, and managed health workforce.The Comprehensive Mental Health Action Plan for 2013-2020 is a commitment by all WHO Member States to take specific actions to promote mental well-being, prevent mental disorders, provide care, enhance recovery, promote human rights and reduce the mortality, morbidity and disability for persons with mental disorders including in older adults. It focuses on 4 key objectives to:

- strengthen effective leadership and governance for mental health;
- provide comprehensive, integrated and responsive mental health and social care services in community-based settings;
- implement strategies for promotion and prevention in mental health; and
- strengthen information systems, evidence and research for mental health.

Depression, psychoses, suicide, epilepsy, dementia and substance use disorders are included in the WHO Mental Health Gap Action Programme (mhGAP) that aims to improve care for mental, neurological and substance use disorders through providing guidance and tools to develop health services in resource-poor areas. The mhGAP package consists of interventions for prevention and management for each of these priority conditions in non-specialized health settings including in those for older people.

Conclusion

To conclude, it can be stated that mental health of older person is a big issue in our society; for that we must take special responsibility for them. From Government side, it should be modified the existing system of policies and made new policy to increase the awareness among peoples for well health of older person those who are above 60 years old. The number of older adults is growing fast all over the world. The socio-economic impact of such demographic changes is adding to overall mental health consequences. WHO is supporting governments to narrow down the service gap for mental health, particularly in resource-poor settings.

REFERENCES

Alexopoulos, G.S., Reynolds, C.F., Bruce, M.L., Katz, I.R., Raue, P.J., Mulsant, B.H. & Ten Have, T. "PROSPECT Group (2009). Reducing suicidal ideation and depression in older primary care patients: 24-month outcomes of the PROSPECT study". *American Journal of Psychiatry*, 166(8), 882-90.

Alvidrez, J., Areán, P., & Stewart, A., (2005). "Psychoeducation to increase psychotherapy entry for older African Americans". *The American Journal of Geriatric Psychiatry*, 13(7), 554-561.

American Psychiatric Association, (2000). *Diagnostic and statistical manual of mental disorders* (4th ed., Text Revision). Washington, DC: Author.

Andresen, E.M., Malmgren, J.A., Carter, W.B., & Patrick, D.L., (1994). "Screening for depression in well older adults: Evaluation of a short form of the CES-D." *American Journal of Preventive Medicine*, 10(2), 77-84.

Areán, P.A., Hegel, M.T., & Reynolds, C.F. (2001). "Treating depression in older medical patients with psychotherapy". *Journal of Clinical Geropsychology*, 7(2), 93-104.

Bartels, S.J., Coakley, E.H., Zubritsky, C., Ware, J.H., Miles, K.M., Areán, P.A. & Levkoff, S.E. for the PRISM-E Investigators, (2004). "Improving access to geriatric mental health services: a randomized trial comparing treatment engagement with integrated versus enhanced referral care for depression, anxiety, and at-risk alcohol use". *American Journal of Psychiatry*, 161, 1455-62.

Website used

http://www.who.int>mediacentre>factsheets/fs381

8

Crimes against the Senior Citizens of the Nation

Jyoti Singh and *Srishti Dey*

Introduction

According to census 2011, there are 104 million elderly persons (aged 60 and above) in India. Normally, males outnumber females in total population. But among population of elderly, the reverse is true, i.e. there are 53 million females and 51 million males. The mean age of the elderly across the cities is 67 years. As per World Bank, the life expectancy has increased from 40 years in 1951 to 64 years in 2011. Three fifth (60%) of the elderly are currently married, while more than one third (38%) are widow/ widower. With declining fertility, coupled with increase in life expectancy, the number of older persons in population of India is expected to increase more than double from 71 million in 2001 to 173 million by 2026.

Traditionally in India, while children pursue education and other career building activities to become economically productive and adults and middle aged engage themselves in earning livelihood and form the working population of the nation, the elderly mostly lead a retired life. All three generations, namely, children, parents and grandparents reside side by side harmoniously in the same household. The elderly get care, support and comfort from their children and grandchildren. With the advent of modernity and globalisation and the accompanying phenomena such as urbanisation and migration, the conventional living style has been changing phenomenally. Number of nuclear families is increasing and more and more elderly are now living alone. The percept of regarding maintenance of elderly as a pious obligation is also wearing off. These changes have increased the need for change in the social, economic and political condition of adults. The change in these demographics has also led to need in change as regards the process of healthy ageing.

In the recent times, adults have been subjected to a wide variety of crimes and have alerted the society to develop increased care and protection mechanisms for them, as per the changing needs of the society. The increasing crimes against elderly are proving to be a growing menace for the Indian society. Senior citizens are most vulnerable to be victim of any crime, since they are soft targets. The cases of crimes against the elderly are on the rise across the country. Today, they are victims of grievous hurt, murder, and abuse and isolated by neighbours, family members and domestic servants.

Recent trends and major crimes against the elderly

The quantitative component of the study conducted by HelpAge India covered the elderly in the age group of 60+years across 9 cities viz. Delhi NCR, Mumbai, Ahemdabad, Kolkata, Bhopal, Chennai, Patna, Hyderabad and Bangalore with a sample size of 100 per city in May, 2011. For the qualitative part, In Depth Interviews (IDI) among legal experts, members of Senior Citizen's Association, Police Officers, medical experts, Social Welfare Officer, Community Based Organizations (CBOs) and Psychologists were carried out by Sigma. In all, 50 IDIs with various target groups were carried out. The findings of the survey were startling:

- Three fifth (60%) of the elderly consider verbal abuse as elder abuse while more than two fifth (48%) feel physical abuse constitutes elder abuse.
- More than one third each of the elderly feel that elder abuse constitutes emotional abuse (37%), showing disrespect (36%) and economic abuse (35%).
- Nearly one fifth (19%) of the elderly feel neglected with 20 per cent of the elderly in the age group of 60-69 years feeling so.
- More than two third (72%) of the elderly feel neglected sometimes while 17 per cent feel neglected everyday.
- Feeling of being neglected stems from the family related factors such as family members not interacting and being busy in their own lives/work.
- More than one fifth (22%) of the elderly have experienced any type of abuse with this being reported highest in Bangalore (44%) followed by Hyderabad (38%) and Bhopal (30%).
- Verbal abuse is the most commonly reported abuse faced by the elderly from lower socio-economic strata while it was neglect

reported by the elderly from higher socio-economic strata last year.

- It is observed that higher cases of elder abuse occur among elderly after 70 years. This trend was also observed among the higher socio-economic strata last year.
- Verbal abuse is reported more in Delhi NCR, Mumbai, Hyderabad and Bangalore while emotional abuse seems to be more in Bangalore.
- In case of emotional abuse, mental torture was reported the most with Mumbai recording the highest (84%). 'Speaking in loud voice' is the highest percentage of abuse in case of verbal abuse.
- Abuse is reported more from the family members, with daughter-in-law and son emerging as the major abusers.
- Abuse by daughter-in-law was reported most in Delhi (100%) followed by Hyderabad (89%), and Bhopal (87%).
- Half of the elderly from the lower socio-economic strata reported facing abuse because of lack of emotional support. Last year among the elderly from higher socio-economic strata, property issues emerged as the most common context for abuse.
- More than two third (68%) of the elderly from the lower socio-economic strata did not take any action when they faced abuse.
- Most (98%) of the elderly reported not filing a complaint against abuse faced.
- One fourth of the elderly who took action (25%) reported discussing about the abuse faced with others in the family or in the neighbourhood or community.
- Among the elderly who registered complaint, two fifth (40%) reported that nothing concrete came out of it. One fifth of the elderly reported that as a result of the complaint, the police carried out home visit.
- More than one fourth (29%) of the elderly in the lower socio-economic strata as compared to nearly half of the elderly (48%) last year (from the higher socio-economic strata) expressed willingness to take concrete action.
- Unwillingness to take any action against abuse stems from the perception among the elderly that—'it would lead to further abuse' and 'sense of shame in the community'.
- Awareness about laws, policies and programmes against elder abuse is low among the elderly from lower socio-economic strata.
- One third (33%) of the elderly are aware of existing laws and programmes against elder abuse.

- Among the elderly who are aware of the laws, policies and programmes, 18 per cent are aware of the Maintenance and Welfare of Parents and Senior Citizen's Act, 11 per cent of the elderly are aware of the National Policy on Older Persons and 12 per cent are aware of the Protection for Women against Domestic Violence Act.
- Awareness of the law enforcing agencies is low as only 5 per cent of the elderly are aware of these.
- Two third (66%) of the elderly feel that role of police/lawyers is supportive in controlling elder abuse.
- More than two fifth (43%) of the elderly think that the police is equipped to handle such cases. The percentage of elderly from lower socio-economic strata who are of the view that the Police Department is equipped to handle cases of elder abuse is higher as compared to the elderly from higher socio-economic strata.
- The major measures to be taken up by the law enforcing agencies suggested by the elderly include 'giving protection' (38%), 'serving notice to the abuser' and 'carrying out home visits' (33% each).
- 'Having steady cash flow' (51%), 'having own property to reduce economic dependency' (48%) and 'making adjustments within family' (35%) are the major measures suggested by the elderly to control elder abuse.
- Low percentage of elderly from lower socio-economic strata reported ever facing crime. The highest percentage is reported by elderly in the age group of 70-79 years (3%).
- Among the major types of crime faced by the elderly, as reported are burglary, molestations and criminal acts with less than one tenth (8%) reporting intimidation.
- Only one third (37%) are willing to take any concrete action for crime.
- Unwillingness to take any concrete action stems from 'being scared of facing further crime' and 'no concrete action'.
- Measures suggested for law enforcing agencies to tackle crime include 'law enforcing agencies should provide protection to the elderly', 'serve notice to the person committing crime' and 'home visits to be made at regular intervals'.
- The measures suggested by the elderly in controlling crime include 'inform about the crime to the Police', 'contact counsellors to help deal with the crime', 'procedure for legal aid should be simple and effective', 'contact Senior Citizen's Association/RWA

for help and guidance' and 'simplify procedure for Police intervention'.

According to a report of the National Crimes Record Bureau, a total of 20,532 cases of IPC crimes against senior citizens were registered during 2015, showing an increase of 9.7 per cent during the year over previous year 2014 (18,714 cases). Out of 20,532 IPC crimes under crime against senior citizens, maximum cases were registered under cheating (1,867 cases) followed by robbery (1,294 cases), murder (1,053 cases) and grievous hurt (949 cases), contributing 9.1 per cent, 6.3 per cent, 5.1 per cent and 4.6 per cent of total such crimes during 2015 respectively. State/UT-wise trends reveal that maximum cases of crime against senior citizens were registered in Maharashtra followed by Madhya Pradesh, Andhra Pradesh and Tamil Nadu accounting for 22.2 per cent (4,561 cases), 16.8 per cent (3,456 cases), 12.1 per cent (2,495 cases) and 9.5 per cent (1,947 cases) of total such cases (20,532 cases) respectively during 2015. A total of 23,615 persons (consisting of 22,252 male and 1,363 female) were arrested under crimes against senior citizens during 2015. Majority of persons arrested for crimes against senior citizens were reported from Madhya Pradesh (5,739) followed by Maharashtra (5,062), Tamil Nadu (2,492), Andhra Pradesh (2,283), Chhattisgarh (1,397) and Uttar Pradesh (966) during 2015.

Crime rate of 20.0 was reported at all India level during 2015. Delhi has reported the maximum rate of such crimes with 108.8 crime rate followed by Madhya Pradesh (60.5), Chhattisgarh (53.7), Andhra Pradesh (51.6), A & N Islands (47.2), Telangana (44.1) and Maharashtra (41.1).

Murder- ***(Incidence: 1,053 Rate 1.0)***

A total of 1,053 cases of murder of senior citizens were registered during 2015. Most of such cases were registered in Maharashtra (167 cases), Tamil Nadu (162 cases), Uttar Pradesh (151 cases) and Madhya Pradesh (106 cases), these States together accounted for 55.6 per cent (586 cases out of 1,053 cases) of total such cases during 2015.

Out of 1,871 persons arrested for murder of elderly people in the country, maximum number of arrested persons were reported in Uttar Pradesh (449) followed by Maharashtra (258), Tamil Nadu (246) and Madhya Pradesh (214).

Attempt to Commit Murder- ***(Incidence: 456 Rate 0.4)***

A total of 456 cases of attempt to commit murder of senior citizens were registered during 2015. Most of such cases were reported in Bihar (94 cases), Tamil Nadu (71 cases) and Maharashtra (62 cases), these States together accounted for 49.8 per cent (227 cases out of 456 cases) of total cases of attempt to commit murder during 2015.

Out of 736 persons arrested for attempt to commit murder of elderly people, maximum arrested persons were reported from Maharashtra (146 persons) followed by Bihar (110 persons) and Tamil Nadu (100 persons) during 2015.

Grievous Hurt - *(Incidence: 949; Rate 0.9)*

A total of 949 cases of grievous hurt of elderly people were registered during 2015. Majority of these cases were registered in Maharashtra (369 cases) and Madhya Pradesh (150 cases), these two States together accounted for 54.7 per cent (519 cases out of 949 cases) of total such cases during 2015. Arrests of 1,509 persons for causing grievous hurt to elderly people were made in the country during 2015. Maximum number of persons arrested for such crime was reported from Maharashtra (594) and Madhya Pradesh (284).

Cheating- *(Incidence: 1,867 Rate 1.8)*

A total of 1,867 cases of cheating where victims were senior citizens, have been registered during 2015. High number of such cases were registered in Maharashtra (627 cases) followed by Telangana (240 cases), Andhra Pradesh (197 cases) and Tamil Nadu (192 cases), these four States together accounted for 67.3 per cent (1,256 cases out of 1,867 cases) of total such cheating cases during 2015.

A total of 1,288 persons were arrested for cheating under crime against elderly persons in the country during 2015. Maximum persons arrested for such crime were reported in Maharashtra (367) followed by Tamil Nadu (168) and Andhra Pradesh (125).

Robbery - (*Incidence: 1,294 Rate 1.3)*

A total of 1,294 cases of robbery under crime against senior citizens were registered in the country during 2015. Majority of such cases were registered in Maharashtra (718 cases) followed by Delhi UT (145 cases) and Karnataka (118), these three States together accounted for 75.8 per cent (981 cases out of 1,294 cases) of total such cases during 2015.

A total of 1,136 persons were arrested for such crime in the country during 2015. Maximum number of persons arrested for such crime was reported from Maharashtra (604) followed by Karnataka (102).

Dacoity - ***(Incidence: 47 Rate Negligible)***

A total of 47 cases of dacoity under crime against senior citizens were registered in the country during 2015, showing an increase of 17.5 per cent during 2015 over 2014 (40 cases). Majority of such cases were registered in Maharashtra (27 cases) accounting for 57.4 per cent of total such cases reported in the country during 2015.

Extortion - ***(Incidence: 94 Rate 0.1)***

94 cases of extortion under crime against senior citizens were registered in the country during 2015, showing an increase of 248.1 per cent during 2015 over 2014 (27 cases). High number of such cases were reported in Andhra Pradesh (28 cases) followed by Maharashtra (19 cases).

Disposal of Cases of Crime against Elderly by Police

- Investigation of a number of cases of crimes against elderly in Delhi, Mumbai and Kolkata remains pending. The consequent delay affects adversely the fate of these cases.
- During the period from 2003 to 2007, average charge sheeting rate of cases of cognizable IPC crime in which senior citizens were victims in Delhi, Mumbai and Kolkata was respectively 52.5 per cent, 40.7 per cent and 49.5 per cent. There is a scope for substantial increase in charge sheeting rate of cases of crime against elderly as is evident from the fact that during 2003, 2004 and 2007 on all-India level, charge sheeting rate, of total number of cases of cognizable IPC crime was 80.1 per cent, 79.8 and 80.1 per cent respectively.
- Average charge sheeting rate in respect of cases of offences against body of senior citizens in Delhi, Mumbai and Kolkata during 2003-07 was 86.5, 80.4 and 90.5 per cent respectively. This is indicative of closer attention that police in these metros gives to offences against life of senior citizens.
- Average charge sheeting rate in respect of cases of crime against property of senior citizens in Delhi, Mumbai and Kolkata during 2003-07 was 28.0, 30.3 and 25.1 per cent respectively. This shows police gives scant attention to these offences and senior citizens suffer a great deal of pecuniary loss due to crimes against their property.
- Average charge sheeting rate in respect of cases of economic crimes in which senior citizens were victims was also low. Thus,

there is a need for much better investigation of cases of crime against property and economic offences.

Disposal of Cases against Senior Citizens by Court

- **Pendency percentage** in Delhi and Mumbai in trial of criminal cases in which senior citizens were victims being 87.2 and 91.2 was enormous and it is matter of immense concern.
- **Average conviction rate** of 24.0 per cent in Delhi for 2003-07 in cases of offences against body was disappointingly low. Corresponding rate of 58.7 per cent in cases relating to property was quite impressive. Corresponding rates in Mumbai were 39.4 per cent and 66.1 per cent respectively.
- Quick disposal of cases by police and courts and higher conviction rates are some of the important factors that facilitate crime control.

3. Causes of Crimes against Senior Citizens

- **Living alone** – Most elderly today live alone after being discarded by their families. Out of those staying with families, more than two third (72%) of the elderly stay with son, while one fourth (23%) stay with spouse and more than one tenth (13%) are living with daughters, all of whom are busy with their jobs and earning livelihood leaving the elderly alone at home most of the times.
- **Modernization and western influence** – With the advancement in science and technology, the world is increasingly shrinking to become a global village. There has been tremendous influence of the western culture on Indian societies that forces the elderly to live alone and take care of themselves on their own, as in the west. Modernization and extreme forms of urbanisation is also a leading cause of crimes against elderly.
- **Unskeptical minds and friendly behaviour** – The people belonging to the elderly section are not very skeptical; they do not usually raise questions on doubtful behaviour of people around them like servants, over friendly strangers and neighbours, relatives, etc. They tend to trust people with ease making them easy targets of crimes.
- **Physically and mentally weak** – A total of 1,435 robbery, dacoity and extortion was reported against the elderly in the year 2015. The reason behind such instances is the fact that they are generally physically and mentally weak and are not able to defend themselves when such attacks occur.

- **Viewed as a liability** – The concept of maintaining a parent out of affection or as a pious obligation is considered as an outdated notion in today's strenuous and hectic schedule. They are rather viewed as a liability, a burden and an unwanted responsibility. Children are allured and drawn to the idea of earning livelihoods for themselves and self-sustenance.
- **Financial dependency** – More than half (52%) of the elderly are illiterate with one fourth (23%) having completed Primary levels and 15 per cent having Middle level education. As regards the last main occupation, one third worked as unskilled workers and 26 per cent were homemakers. One fifth (21%) of the elderly are currently engaged in any economic activity with Chennai reporting the highest (38%) and Delhi NCR the lowest (7%). One fourth of the elderly in the age group of 60-69 years and less than one fifth (18%) in the age group of 70-79 years are currently engaged in any economic activity. More than one fourth (29%) of the elderly currently economically active are petty traders and 13 per cent are shop owners. The average monthly household income of the elderly is Rs. 6269. About 30 per cent of the elderly have a monthly household income in the range of Rs 2501-5000. More than half (55%) of the elderly have remittance from children as the main source of income and more than one third (35%), pension. These facts clearly indicate towards the financial dependency of the elderly on their children, which is also a matter of concern and major cause of crimes against the elderly.
- **Breakdown of Joint family system** – The traditional joint family system in India has undergone both structural and functional changes. This disintegration has occurred due to several reasons and has extensively affected the lives of elderly in India.
- **Other factors** –
  I. Abusers have learned from behaviours of others around them that violence is a way to solve problems or obtain a desired outcome.
  II. Abusers feel that they do not receive enough benefit from their relationship with the elderly person, so they resort to violence in an effort to obtain their fair share.
  III. A combination of background and current factors, such as recent conflicts and a family history of "solving" problems through violence influences the relationship.
  IV. Abusers use a pattern of coercive tactics to gain and maintain power and control in a relationship.

Possible Safeguards and Available Remedies

The following measures and safeguards were suggested by Group for Economic & Social Studies (GESS) in their report titled "RISING CRIMES AGAINST ELDERLY PEOPLE AND RESPONSIBILITY OF POLICE IN METROS" submitted to the BUREAU OF POLICE RESEARCH AND DEVELOPMENT, Ministry of Home Affairs, and Government of India—

Some Safeguards for the Elderly

- Parents cannot be evicted from a house without due process of the law.
- Under Section 125 of the CrPC, a person not having sufficient means can claim maintenance from his children.
- If children or relatives neglect or refuse to maintain a senior citizen unable to maintain himself/herself, they can be ordered to pay a monthly allowance to such senior citizen under the Maintenance and Welfare of Parents and Senior Citizens Act, 2007.
- The Hindu Adoptions and Maintenance Act provides that an aged parent can demand maintenance from children.
- The Domestic Violence Act also provides parents with the right to seek relief from any kind of abuse.
- Based on provisions of Article 41 of the Constitution of India and obligations under various UN backed international agreements, the National Policy on Older Persons (NPOP) was announced in January 1999. It identifies a number of areas of intervention — financial, health care, nutrition, shelter, education, welfare and protection of life & property — for the well-being of older persons. National Council for Older Persons (NCOP) has been constituted to operationalise the NPOP.
- Government of India passed Maintenance and Welfare of Parents and Senior Citizens Act, 2007. The features of this act are—(a) Maintenance of parents and senior citizens. (b) Places are legal obligation on children and relatives to maintain the parents and senior citizens. (c) Government should set up maintenance tribunals. (d) Government should establish old age homes in all the districts with the help of Non-Governmental Organizations. (e) Helpline service should be started in bigger cities. (f) The elderly should be provided legal aid services. (g) Friendly visit should be started by the police.
- The National Social Assistance Programme (1995), provides financial security to poor older people. There are various other

schemes of Government that ensures health security, shelter, various concessions, construction of old age homes etc.

Security Arrangements for Elderly

When overall crime situation in an area is well under control, crime against elderly and other weaker sections is less. When crime situation deteriorates, these sections are hit hardest. At the same time, special crime control measures are necessary for the protection of aged persons in view of the problems they face due to their frailty/disabilities and lonely lives, they are compelled to lead. It appears that while Delhi has a fairly comprehensive and formal action plan for providing protection and security to its senior citizens, such plans for Mumbai, Kolkata and Chennai, are yet to be evolved. Special crime control measures for elderly include:

- Senior Citizens Security Cells;
- Senior Citizens Toll-Free Help-lines;
- Registration with police of senior citizens living alone for exercising extra vigilance in relation to them through sensitised beat patrols, police patrol vans and volunteers from local communities, enrolled as special police officers;
- Special drives for verification of antecedents of servants, drivers and other domestic helps as also of tenants;
- Sensitisation of people/Resident Welfare Associations (RWAs) regarding safety measures;
- Counselling of senior citizens;
- Mobilisation of members of public and NGOs/voluntary organisations such as Help Age, Age Well, Abhaash, Akaash, youth clubs, women groups, etc. for providing emotional support to lonely citizens; and
- Encouraging setting up of senior citizens organisations. Unfortunately, despite these special security measures, crime against elderly is a chilling recurring feature.

Suggestions of Police for Resident Welfare Associations (RWAs) and NGOs

Suggestions given by police personnel of four metros during this study include:

- RWAs should play active role in resolving minor disputes in which senior citizens are involved;

- They should be more effective in improving police-public relationships;
- They should convince senior citizens to follow police advisories concerning safety and security matters, verification of antecedents of their domestic helps and tenants, and registration with police, and
- They should help senior citizens to organise their own groups for solving their problems mutually.

During this study it was found that 85 per cent of respondents in Delhi, 63 per cent in Mumbai, 67 per cent in Kolkata and 65 per cent in Chennai were not satisfied with the current arrangements for protection and security of senior citizens. Their suggestions for improving security of elderly include:

1. Strengthening of beat police system,
2. More frequent visits of beat constables for those who are living alone or with spouses,
3. Foot patrolling both during daytime and night,
4. Each police station should have complete record of all senior citizens whether staying alone or in joint families in its area,
5. More frequent interaction between police and residents of the area, and
6. Fixation of responsibility for lapses due to which each serious incident of crime takes place and proper follow up action on reports of inquiries conducted for this purpose.

Empowerment of Elderly

- **Need for Literacy**: There is a need to introduce literacy programmes for older persons, which would reduce their vulnerability to exploitation and help in strengthening their knowledge of their rights, access to entitlements and services, capacity to overcome discrimination and ability to resist violence.
- **Information and education material** relevant to the lives and security of older people should be developed and translated in local languages and widely disseminated.
- **T.V. Channel for Elderly**: Loneliness and passing time are the pivotal problems of the aged. For literacy and recreation of the elderly, there is a need for a special T.V. channel. Alternatively, *Doordashan* should run regularly dedicated programmes for literacy and recreation of elderly.

- **Job Reservations for Elderly**: Government of India, State Governments, Union Territory Administrations, local bodies, academic institutions, public sector undertakings and private sector establishments should identify lighter jobs to which elder citizens can be recruited and earmark a portion of these jobs for qualified, needy, physically and mentally fit senior citizens, who are willing for employment.

Administrative Measures

- **Reorganisation of Mega City Police:** Police set-up of each metro should be urgently reviewed to reorganise it to make it better face its current and future challenges and to meet expectations of the people. This will automatically improve security for all including elderly. At present police in metro is overstretched. For example, Dwarka area in Delhi has one police station, which has to look after 6.5 lakh people.
- **Senior Citizen Cells:** Each police headquarters and each district police office of the metro should have a senior citizen cell.
- **Police Station-wise Security Scheme:** Each police station should prepare and update regularly schemes for protection of elderly in the context of local requirements, which should, *inter alia*, provide for patrolling both during day and night. Police should get **extra functional and supervisory staff** needed for enforcing the scheme.
- **Data Base:** Police should maintain and regularly update data base about elderly and obtain feedback about security arrangements in force for elderly.
- **Training and Re-orientation of Staff:** Police personnel should also be given training in dealing with and taking care of elderly.
- **Fast Tracking of Investigations and Trials of Cases:** Investigations and trials of criminal cases in which senior citizens are victims, as also trials of civil cases in which senior citizens are parties should be fast-tracked. Convicts in criminal cases, in which elderly are victims, should be awarded exemplary punishments.
- **Better and Scientific Investigation:** Investigation of cases of property and economic offences in which senior citizens are victims needs to be improved substantially as charge-sheeting rates in respect of them are low.
- **Co-option of Security and Placement Agencies:** The security and placement agencies should be encouraged to provide guards and

domestic helps having skill for taking care of elderly and cleared from security angle so that well-to-do senior citizens, who are at greater security risks, can have qualified and reliable personal and security staff.

- **Accountability:** Enquiries should be held to fix responsibility for lapses due to which each serious incident of crime against elderly takes place and suitable remedial measures/action should be instituted/taken in the light of result of these enquiries. At the same time, police personnel and members of public who help in prevention and detection of crime against elderly should be handsomely rewarded/recognised.
- **Crime Statistics:** National Crime Record Bureau should publish statistics relating to crime against elderly and elder abuse as a part of its annual publication, "Crime in India", to facilitate formulation of strategies to combat this crime/abuse.
- **Population Statistics:** Office of Registrar General of India may consider publication of mid-year population estimates of elderly people annually to give an idea of the magnitudes of problems of older persons.
- **Financial Security:** There is a strong case for a large hike in amount of old age pension to ameliorate the lot of destitute elderly. This rate should be periodically reviewed.
- **Mobility Risk:** Police, town planners, road engineers and public transport administrators should evolve and implement measures to minimize mobility risk of elderly. Architects should keep in mind the need of safety, security and comfort of elderly while designing houses and institutions.

Statutory and Policy Measures

- **Need for Research:** Sustained multidimensional research and data gathering on problems of elderly and old age that would help in devising and implementing cost-effective measures for well-being and protection of elderly and provision of old age security should be undertaken and generously funded by Central Government.
- **Institutional Arrangements:** Though there are clear symptoms of collapsing of traditional support system for elderly, National Policy on Old Persons (NPOP) assumes that social security role of family is continuing. It is high time for modifying this assumption and making efforts through public-private participation for putting in place affordable institutional arrangements for protection and care

of non-destitute elderly. Incentives may also be considered for families and hoteliers who are willing to take senior citizens on affordable rates as paying guests.

- **Legislative Measures:** A special law needs to be enacted centrally to supplement/replace the Maintenance and Welfare of Parents and Senior Citizen Act, 2007 to deal comprehensively with the problems of crime against elderly and elder abuse including domestic violence and to provide relief to victims of such crime and abuse. The proposed law should specify responsibilities of police, resident welfare associations, managements of homes/ other institutional caregivers to elderly and local bodies *vis-à-vis* elderly. This law should provide for stern punishments for convicts in cases of crime against older persons as also for regulation and inspection of old-age homes. The Motor Vehicle Act may be amended to reduce the mobility risk for older persons.
- **Sensitisation of Younger Generation:** School curricula should include material that inculcates sensitivity and values, which promote proper attitude for care and respect for elderly and develop skills for giving care and emotional support to elderly.

Civil Society Institutions/Resident Welfare Associations

- **Need for Better Security Precautions for RWAs**: RWAs should arrange for better local area security—both physical and manual. They should regulate entry of outsiders including casual workers, vendors and tradesmen in their premises more effectively.
- **Dispute Redressal:** They should play active role in resolving minor problems of senior citizens.
- **Security Vetting of Tradesmen and Domestic Helps:** RWAs should provide a panel of verified electricians, plumbers and other tradesmen for service in their premises. They should have arrangements with registered firms/placement agencies for providing reliable domestic help to houses in their premises.
- **Sensitisation of Residents about Security Matters:** RWAs should launch from time to time drives to convince senior citizens and other residents to follow advisories concerning safety and security matters, verification of antecedents of their domestic helps and tenants, and registration with police.
- **Self Help Groups:** RWAs, NGOs, youth clubs, and women groups should help senior citizens to organise their own groups/ organisations involving persons from different walks of life like doctors, lawyers, security experts, etc. so that their expertise can

be of use to them in solving their problems mutually. State Governments should partly fund senior citizens groups/ organisations.

- **Community Liaison Groups:** They should also organize volunteers to pay regular visits to senior citizens to attend to their emotional needs and to run errands for them.
- **Neighbourhood Watch Schemes:** RWAs, Senior Citizen's Welfare Associations, Senior Citizen's Neighborhood Societies should evolve and enforce neighbourhood watch schemes.

Conclusion

India is one of the largest growing economies in the world. The Indian society has also been drastically changing at a very rapid rate. The elderly are now victims of mistreatment, cruelty, violence, neglect, exploitation, manipulation, verbal and physical abuse and several other heinous crimes. The UN Population Fund India's report observes that "*Everyone has a part to play for the well-being of the elderly, including the Government and civil society, communities and families...*". Many older people in India are not aware about their basic human rights due to high occurrence of illiteracy and lack of alertness. Surveys have found that one out of every six older person living in urban India are not obtaining proper nutrition, one out of every three older persons does not obtain sufficient health care or medicine and one out of two older persons do not receive due respect or good conduct from family members or people in general. It is now need of the hour to change the situation and provide the elderly better care protection and comfort.

REFERENCES

Box, S.C., Hale and G. Andrews, (1998). "Explaining fear of Crime", *British Journal of Criminology*, 28 (3), 340, 356.

Bagga, Amrita and Anuradha Sakurkar, (2011). "Abuse and Violence in the Lives of Older Women: It's Impact on their mental health", *Help Age India-Research & Development Journal*, 173 (3), 7-19.

Chaturvedi, Murlidhar, (2007), *Criminology and Penalogy*, Allahabad Law Agency, Allahabad, p. 216.

Help Age India (2011). *Elder Abuse & Crime in India*. New Delhi.

Jackson, J. (2009). "A Psychological Perspective on Vulnerability in the Fear of Crime". *Psychology, Crime and Law*, 15(4), 365-390.

Madhava Soma Sundaram, P., (1996). "Experience of Fear of Crime and Victimization". *Indian Journal of Criminology*, 24 (1 & 2) Jan. & July, 1996.

National Crime Records Bureau (2001-2010, 2015). *Crime in India Report*. New Delhi.

9

Violence Against Older Women

Consequences and Preventive Measures

Suraj Sharma, Nitul Das and *Seema R. Nambiar*

Introduction

Old age comprises "the later part of life; the period of life after youth and middle age." At what age old age begins cannot be universally defined because it differs according to the context. Most developed countries have accepted the chronological age of 50 years as a definition of 'elderly' or older person. The United Nations has agreed that 65+ years may be usually denoted as old age and this is the first attempt at an international definition of old age. However, for its study of old age in Africa, the World Health Organization (WHO) set 55 as the beginning of old age. At the same time, the WHO recognized that the developing world often defines old age, not by years, but by new roles, loss of previous roles, or inability to make active contributions to society.

Most developed countries have accepted the chronological age of 65 years as a definition of 'elderly' or older person, but like many westernized concepts, this does not adapt well to the situation in Africa. While this definition is somewhat arbitrary, it is many times associated with the age at which one can begin to receive pension benefits. At the moment, there is no United Nations standard numerical criterion, but the UN agreed cut off is 60+ years to refer to the older population.

Violence against older women is widespread but mostly hidden. It occurs in numerous, often intersecting ways, inflicted by a variety of perpetrators including intimate partners or spouses, family members, caregivers both in homes and institutional settings, and community members. Yet reliable, comprehensive data on how often it occurs—among whom, by whom, and what its associated personal and economic costs are—don't exist, despite research showing that trauma induced by abuse across the lifespan has a devastating impact on older women. The World Health Organization (WHO) regards as "elder abuse", harm to a person aged 60 or older, through any single or repeated act, including physical or sexual violence, emotional or financial abuse, neglect and abandonment. Accumulated gender disparities experienced over a lifetime means women are more vulnerable to violence, as they are to poverty, in their later years. But "elder abuse" lacks a specific gender lens and excludes women beyond reproductive age but not yet considered "old" in their specific cultural context.

Causes

1. **Gender Inequality and Ageism:** The Beijing Declaration underscored the reality that across the globe, women's full and equal participation in society is prevented and their opportunities are restricted "by discriminatory attitudes, unjust social and economic structures, and a lack of resources" throughout their entire lifespan. Older age adds another layer of discrimination and deprivation. Combined, age and gender discrimination can lead to a lifetime of greater likelihood of poverty, limited access to protective resources, and heightened risk of violence and abuse.
2. **Socio-Political Causes:** The prevalence of various socio-political disturbances/situations in different parts of the world including India which leaves, above all the children and older women vulnerable. This leaves them in a situation where they are unable to take control of the situation as a result the anti-social elements tend to exploit them in various ways. The conflict situations has seen incidents like these where the older women are subjected to different types of violence.
3. **Economic Deprivation:** In both developed and developing countries, older women are more likely than their male counterparts to be poorer. Living in poverty augments older women's vulnerability to violence, limiting their ability to leave an abusive partner or household due to limited economic independence. The majority (80%) of the world's older people do not have access to any form of pension. Access to land is one of the fundamental economic, social, and cultural rights protected under various international treaties and national constitutions, yet women own only 1 to 2 per cent of all land worldwide.
4. **Isolation from family and friends:** Older women who are isolated from friends, family, and community have a threefold risk of

exploitation and limited to no access to services or support in the event they experience violence or abuse.

5. **Cognitive decline and dementia:** Of all people with dementia—most of whom are women—about half experience some form of abuse. Older women with dementia are especially vulnerable, as it may prevent them from seeking help for abuse or cause the recipients of reports to question their veracity. Globally, the rate of people with dementia being abused by their caregivers is high, ranging from prevalence of 34 per cent to 62 per cent. In regions where belief in *witchcraft* is strong, older women with cognitive decline or severe dementia are sometimes accused of being witches, and are subjected to extreme physical and emotional violence and/or social exclusion.
6. **Disability and care dependency:** Women and girls with disabilities of all ages are subjected to violence and abuse at alarmingly high rates, as high as 80 per cent over the course of their lifetimes. Disability can be an added risk factor for older women, who may acquire an age-related disability.

Consequences

1. For older survivors of sexual assault, the health consequences and resulting injuries are often more severe. Older women who had more recent assaults were more likely to sustain genital or other injury and more frequently required medical treatment. Older women with a history of repeated experiences of sexual assault demonstrated a two to threefold risk of arthritis and breast cancer compared to older women without a history of assault.
2. Violence against older woman reduces employee productivity, the ability of survivors to maintain stable jobs, and in severe cases, forces survivors to miss work, as older woman whose labour force participation has increased since 1990 in all regions of the world.
3. A significant proportion of the global agricultural workforce is above the age of 55, with a majority of older women who are economically active citing agriculture as their primary source of income (62% in Asia and 59% in sub-Saharan Africa). Lost productivity due to injury from violence and abuse may therefore impact the agricultural output of many low- and middle-income countries.
4. Poor nutritional status and malnutrition contribute to progressive decline in health, reduced physical and cognitive functional

status, increased utilization of health care services, premature institutionalization, and increased mortality.

Preventive measures

Based on a combination of age and gender discrimination, older women are routinely denied access to health services, care, support for independent living, education, social security, information, appropriate housing, financial services, employment, transport, and other facets of economic, social, and community life. Such exclusion undermines the development of protective factors against violence and heightens their risk for violence and abuse. This reality has implications for decisions and actions that must be taken at the national policy, institutional, and community levels.

Policy levels

(a) Work with pertinent ministries or policymakers to ensure proposed legislation, as well as current legal and customary practices, do not discriminate against individuals based on age, including laws or informal practices that provide differential treatment to older women than older men.

(b) Work with governments to revise existing laws on inheritance, land rights, and tenure of property to ensure that older women are not excluded from the right to own land or hold property under their own name.

(c) Encourage governments to develop policies and take all appropriate measures (including awareness campaigns) to combat ageism and sexism, as well as foster intergenerational cooperation and positive images of aging, to promote the respectful treatment of older women.

(d) Ensure that the legal definitions of "rape" and "sexual assault" are relevant to all people—regardless of age or gender. Definitions of sexual violence should recognize any unwanted or forced sexual contact and not just forced penetration. For example, many cases of sexual violence against older women involve forced genital touching, which can degrade a survivor's dignity and cause significant psychological trauma.

(e) Work with ministries of justice and other policymakers to ensure all forms of violence and abuse experienced by women in older age are identified as crimes and that they are reported, investigated, and when appropriate, prosecuted.

(f) Engage older women and men in the development of policies and structures that articulate and protect their rights. This may be particularly important for those from underrepresented and marginalized groups, such as indigenous, this engagement helps to ensure that their voices are heard and that the full spectrum of their specific needs and experiences can be recognized and, ideally, addressed through policy instruments and relevant policy actions.

Community level

(a) Consultations with stakeholders are crucial for designing effective programmes. Work with older women and men, listen to their experiences, and build bridges between older adults and feminist and other social justice organizations in the community. By engaging older women as leaders in their communities, the project combats age and gender discrimination and promotes a positive view of older women.

(b) Involve communities, including religious and other leaders, to stimulate change in the social norms that perpetuate ageism, sexism, and other forms of discrimination. These prevailing attitudes contribute to the maltreatment of older women, such as unreported violence or accusations of witchcraft fuelled by superstitions and traditional beliefs.

(c) Support projects that promote participation, local empowerment, responsiveness to demand, greater downward accountability, and enhanced local capacity—i.e. "community driven development" that is inclusive of older persons. This can build the financial and social empowerment of marginalized groups.

(d) Work with community leaders and members to promote older women's property rights, including: their ability to own, use, occupy, transfer, sell, inherit, and distribute land and other property; allowing older women to participate in the redistribution of land and in property programmes on an equal basis with others and ensure they are not arbitrarily or unlawfully deprived of their property; and eliminating traditional widowhood practices that deprive women of property and inheritance rights and in some cases can lead to their death or forced marriage. When possible, raise awareness about national laws creating equal property rights between men and women and effective application.

Conclusion

It can be said that women can be victims of violence over the ages especially the older women. It is seen that in all the studies related to the violence on women often the study does not include in any way the older women and are sidelined. In order to bring a holistic change in the society regarding the control of violence against women, the issue of violence on the older women needs to be taken care of. This will include a systematic and extensive study of the issues related to the matter of violence against older women. The issue leaves a massive negative impact on the elderly women which therefore puts the society at an unstable situation. In order to mitigate this issue it is also pertinent to deal it in the government level by formulating suitable legislation related to geriatric care and strict implementation of existing law and order with special emphasis on the elderly women. In the community level too there is also an urgent need to have a sensitive attitude towards the older people and nurture an inclusive and holistic mentality.

REFERENCES

https://en.wikipedia.org/wiki/Old_age

https://blogs.worldbank.org/voices/violence-against-older-women-widespread-untallied

http://www.helpage.org/what-we-do/rights/violence-against-older-women/

https://www.ncbi.nlm.nih.gov/pmc/articles/PMC3130511/

10
National and International Organizations Working for Older Persons

Jayanta Thakuria, Meisuangdai Gonmei and *Dipak Sarkar*

Introduction

Just as there are no clear definition of childhood or youth, there are no clear definition of the old age at which the mid-life phase of adulthood ends and later life begins. The social definition of old age varies from society to society and over time. Old age refers to ages nearing or surpassing the life expectancy of human beings, and is thus the end of the human life cycle. Old age comprises "the later part of life; the period of life after youth and middle age, usually with reference to deterioration". At what age old age begins cannot be universally defined because it differs according to the context. Most developed countries have accepted the chronological age of 50 years as a definition of 'elderly' or older person. The United Nations has agreed that 65+ years may be usually denoted as old age and this is the first attempt at an international definition of old age.

Organizations: For helping and giving assistance to the older person various type of international and national organization are there, some of them are discussed below –

International Organizations: An international organization is an organization with an international membership, scope, or presence.

WHO: World Health Organization is an international organization, which also work for old age person. On December 14, 1990, the United Nations General Assembly voted to establish October 1 as the International Day of Older Persons and for the first time on October 1, 1991, the holiday was observed. In 2014, Governments around the world adopted a resolution at the Economic and Social Council that recognized ageism as "the common source of, the justification for and the driving force behind age discrimination." 2017's UNIDOP main theme underscores the link between tapping the talents and contributions of older persons and achieving the implementation of the 2030 Agenda and the Madrid International Plan of Action on Ageing, which is currently undergoing its third review and appraisal process. The objectives of the 2017 UNIDOP are –

- Enabling conditions/measures that influence the readiness of older persons to participate including securing healthcare, regular income, legal protection and access to financial services.
- Pathways/means to facilitate contributions and participation in old age, including technology, education and lifelong learning, access to information, as well as overcoming barriers that exclude or discriminate against older persons.

International NGOs: A non-governmental organization (NGO) is any non-profit, voluntary citizens' group which is organized on a local, national or international level. Non-Governmental Organizations are institutions, recognized by governments as non-profit or welfare oriented, which play a key role as advocates, service providers, activists and researchers on a range of issues pertaining to human and social development. There are numerous INGOs and some of them are cited below—

Age International: Age International is a charity, helping older people to live with dignity. Age International support older people in developing countries as well as some of the poorest countries by improving livelihood, health and healthcare; providing age friendly emergency relief, and by challenging attitudes, influencing decision makers and changing policies.

Age International's main strategy

- Reducing poverty.
- Improving health.
- Protecting and promoting rights.
- Responding to emergencies.

Here are just some of the things that Age International does to help grandparents—

- Eye care and free cataract operations.
- Giving out glasses, walking sticks and hearing aids.

- Creating pensions where they don't exist, and helping people to claim them where they do.
- Setting up micro-credit schemes and giving training so older. people can run their own businesses.
- Providing age-friendly aid during emergencies.

Help Age International: Help Age International is an international NGO that helps older people claim their rights, challenge discrimination, and overcome poverty, so that they can lead dignified, secure, active and healthy lives.

Strategies of Help Age International: (For the period of 2015-20)**:** They mainly focus on where every older woman and man can say that—

- I have the income I need.
- I enjoy the best possible health and care, well-being and dignity.
- I am safe and secure, free from all forms of discrimination, violence and abuse.
- My voice is heard.

The following are some of the activities or the works which are being carried out by the Help Age International:

- Provide direct assistance, where necessary, to poor and vulnerable older people.
- Build the capacity of key actors (older people, policymakers and service providers) to work together to develop policy and put changes into practice.
- Advocate for change in policy, practice and behaviours directly, via international instruments and bodies, and influencing global debates related to ageing.
- Strengthen the voice of people to influence policy by campaigning for change and implementation, and increasing the visibility of older women and men in society.
- Make the case by building strong evidence, becoming a thought leader and a knowledge hub.

National Organizations: National organizations are those organization which work in national level only. In India there also have some organizations which help the older person of our country.

Increasing proportion of ageing population, a global phenomenon, has hit Indian shores as well. People are living longer. According to 1999 National Policy for Older Persons, expectation of life at birth for males has shown a steady rise from 42 years in 1951-60 to 58 years in 1986-90, it is projected to be 67 years in 2011-16, an increase of about 9 years in a twenty five year period (1986-90 to 2011-16). In the case of females, the increase in expectation of life has been higher—about 11 years during the same period, from 58 years in 1986-90 to 69 year in 2011-16. At age 60 too, the expectation of life shows a steady rise and is a little higher for women. In 1989-93, it was 15 years for males and 16 years for females.

The following table shows the increasing rate of old age person in India.

Year	Male	Female	Total	Growth rate (rounded)
2001	34.94	35.75	70.69	
2006	40.75	42.83	83.58	15 %
2011	48.14	50.33	98.47	18%
2016	58.11	59.99	118.10	20%
2021	70.60	72.65	143.24	21%

Source: Ministry of Social Justice and Empowerment.

For the well-being and support of such a huge number of old age person GOI and some national level NGOs take various initiatives, and some of them are listed below:

Help Age India: Help Age India is a leading charity in India working with and for disadvantaged elderly for nearly 4 decades. It was set up in 1978 and is registered under the Societies' Registration Act of 1860. The aim is to serve elder needs in a holistic manner, enabling them to live active, dignified and healthier lives. Following are some of the work carried out for the welfare and development programme for the old age person:

- Mobile health care.
- Cataract surgeries.
- Physiocare.
- Cancer care.
- Support a grant.
- Old age home.
- Livelihood support.
- Elder helpline.

Dada Dadi: The Dada-Dadi is a non-profit service and advocacy organization headquartered at Chandigarh India. Registered with Registrar of Societies at Chandigarh, India. Registration No: 4040 of 2009.

Dada-Dadi brings together non-profit organizations, businesses and government to develop creative solutions that improve the lives of all older adults. To improve the lives of older, the following are the mission of this organization—

- Social and economic justice.
- Respect and caring for all.
- Innovation.
- Excellence and integrity.
- Health education programme,
- Dada Dadi Medicare Matters,

Despite of above type of NGOs programme, there also have some Governmental policies and programme which help the old age person live happily. One of the main Governmental policy is mentioned below:

National Policy for Old Age Person (1999): The National Policy on Older Persons was announced by the government in 1999, declared as the International Year of Older Persons by the UN. The year 2000 has been declared as the National Year of Older Persons by the Government of India. The decision to frame a policy for older persons was first mooted in the 1980s, following the World Assembly on Ageing held at Vienna in 1982. In 1987-88, an Inter-Ministerial Committee was constituted by the GoI for this purpose. Principal Areas of Intervention and Action Strategies taken up by the national policy for old age person:

- Financial security.
- Health Care and Nutrition.
- Shelter.
- Education.
- Welfare.
- Protection of Life and Property.

Other Areas of Action such as:

- Non-Governmental Organizations.
- Realizing the Potential.
- Family.
- Research.
- Training of Manpower.
- Media.

National Policy on Senior Citizens 2011: The foundation of the new policy, known as the "National Policy for Senior Citizens 2011" is based on several factors. These include the demographic explosion among the elderly, the changing economy and social milieu, advancement in medical research, science and technology and high levels of destitution among the elderly rural poor (51 million elderly live below the poverty line). A higher proportion of elderly women than men experience loneliness and are dependent on children. Social deprivations and exclusion, privatization of health services and changing pattern of morbidity affect the elderly. All those of 60 years and above are senior citizens. This policy addresses issues concerning senior citizens living in urban and rural areas, special needs of the old men and women. In principle, the policy values an age integrated society. It will endeavour to strengthen integration between generations, facilitate interaction between the old and the young as well as strengthen bonds between different age groups.

Areas of working: (1) Income security in old age (2) Health care, (3) Safety and Security (4) Housing, (5) Productive Ageing and (6) Welfare

Conclusion

In fact effortless contribution has been done by various organizations in different level such as national as well as international through different agencies for the welfare of the older persons as a whole by carrying out different beneficial activities. Nevertheless, undoubtedly there are still a good number of older persons all over the world who have being deprived from those facilities which are provided by different organizations. Therefore, more effort may be given by the concerns organizations for the well-being of the older persons. "A society for all ages encompasses the goal of providing older persons with the opportunity to continue contributing to society. To work towards this goal, it is necessary to remove whatever excludes or discriminates against them".

REFERENCES

government of India (1999), *National Policy for Older Person 1999.*

http://www.helpage.org/who-we-are/our-values-and-ambitions/

http://dadadadi.org/programs.html

http://vikaspedia.in/social-welfare/senior-citizens-welfare/policies-and-acts-1/policies-and-acts#section-4

www.ageinternational.org.uk

www.who.int/ageing/global-strategy/en/

Section-III:
Elderly Care and Social Work Intervention

11
Geriatric Social Work Practice:
A Case Study of an Elderly Woman Tea Plantation Worker

Barsha Kalita and *Kaivalya T. Desai*

Introduction

Tea Industry is one of the major industries of India. After British annexed Assam, it discovered the tea plantation as the new avenue for investment of capital and exploitation of resources. However, with the growth of tea plantations, the need for labourers increased. Due to lack of local labourers, labourers were imported from drought-stricken tribal areas of central India. Initially slavery was practiced, which gradually changed to indentured and *Dhubri* system (Chatterjee & Das, 1981). Over the years, the condition of the labourers has improved to a certain extent but still these people struggle to meet their basic needs. They are deprived of safe drinking water, crèches, schools, health facilities, sanitation, proper housing facilities, low wages and delays in payment of wages. Workers face various social, economic as well as health problems in tea plantations (Borah, 2013). The condition of women and elderly tea plantation workers are further deplorable and need immediate attention. Tea plantation is another site of patriarchal society where women do not have any special identity. Women are socialized in such a way that they accept their exploitation without protest. Their ignorance, lack of skills and non-assertive nature makes them submissive both at the place of work and in family life (Bhadra, 1985). Moreover, elderly people in tea plantations have to suffer from various socio-economic problems and health issues along with neglect and deprivation. After their retirement they get a lump-sum amount in the name of provident fund, they lose ownership of the house allotted to them; they struggle to manage basic expenses, fail to access health facilities and have to lead a dependent life.

In a study conducted titled, "The health and well-being of older people and their families in the tea estate of Sri Lanka" (2005), it was depicted how elderly people in tea plantation suffer from various social problems like lack of security, neglect by children, dependency, losing their voice, giving up comfort, conflict with youth and children, feeling lack of respect and developing frustration. Further, they also fail to satisfy their needs, become destitute, lose ownership of house, get abused, are forced to look out for work and lose support or help. Elderly people in tea plantations also suffer from various health issues due to their food habits, lifestyle and hard work throughout their life. These factors also take a toll on their mental and emotional health (Perera & Holmes, 2005). Thus, there is a need to understand the issues and problems of elderly people in tea plantations since there is hardly any study emphasizing on the situation of the elderly. The elderly people in tea plantations need social work intervention for leading a dignified life, free from deprivation and abuse.

Methodology

This chapter is based on a research that attempted to understand the life of elderly tea plantation labourers within a gendered space. Further the chapter attempts to highlight the plausible role that social workerscan play by helping them cope with their everyday challenges, and by providing emotional and physical support. Thus, in order to get an in-depth understanding of the lived experiences of elderly women tea plantation labourers, a qualitative approach was adopted. Case study method was adopted to collect data. Case study helps to examine contemporary real-life situations. It provides a detailed contextual analysis of a limited number of events or conditions. Unstructured, open-ended interviews were conducted to collect data from the elderly women tea plantation labourers. An in-depth field study and prolonged interaction helped in interacting with these women, who opened up about their joys and sorrows. Further, a field diary was maintained to record the observations. This chapter highlights the case study of one elderly woman tea plantation labourer.

The study area selected was Durrung tea estate of Sonitpur District in Brahmaputra Valley. The main population of the area comprises of *Assamese, Bengalis,Gorkhas* and *Adivasis*. Adivasi community is composed of *Mundas, Santhals, Kurukh, Gonds, Kharia, Bhumij, Tanti, Saora* and dozens of motley group of tribes which forms a significant portion accounting for nearly one-third of the district's population or if taken as a whole the largest community in the district with over 6,00,000 people. The sample of the study was selected from Durrung Tea estate of Sonitpur District.

Findings of the study

The findings have been depicted through a case study of a 65 years old woman tea plantation labourer of Durrung tea estate. The case reveals the issues faced by elderly women in tea plantation labourers in general as well as some specific to this particular woman.

Reena is a 65 year old retired woman. She is an old frail lady who walks around the labour lines with the help of a walking stick, draping a white *saree* over her bare body. Years of working have led to her hunch back and she finds it difficult to stand straight. Her ancestors were brought from Jharkhand but she has never been there. Being a daughter in her family she never received education. Due to non-availability of schools in close proximity and lesser emphasis on girls' education, her parents never felt the need to send her to school. Rather she was taught the household responsibilities which her parents felt will lead to her happy married life. At the age of 15 she was married off to her husband who was a permanent worker at that time in Durrung tea estate. She was too young to understand about marriage and her memory does not have much recollection about her marriage. But she clearly remembers that it was an arranged marriage without her consent. Her parents did not ask her opinion before getting her married since they did not think it was necessary. At a young age she had to undertake the responsibility of her family. Her in-laws were supportive and thus she did not find much problem in adjusting to her new life. Initial discomfort, stress to manage household responsibilities and fear of committing mistakes gradually reduced. Her husband was much elder to her so he used to understand her. After few years of her marriage, she gave birth to a daughter then to a son. She had a happy family though occasional challenges did come in their lives. After her son's birth, she decided to join work and in consultation with her husband and in-laws she joined as *faltu* labourer. After few years her father-in-law expired and soon afterwards her mother-in-law also expired. Her mother-in-law was a permanent worker, so after her death, she got the permanent post. Since then she had been working in the garden for more than thirty years.

Years of working had made her apt in plucking and also added lots of memories. When she joined work, there were plenty of tea leaves and at times she used to collect up to 100 kgs of leaves. But with time due to change in weather the quantity of leaves reduced. Along with plucking she also used to do other work like cutting stems, cleaning drain, digging land, etc. Earlier the managers were also very strict and sometimes used to scold without any reason but managers kept on changing and at present the manager does not deal with the labourers directly. She has retired now. It has been five years since retirement. She transferred her permanent post and the house provided from the management to her daughter. She is presently staying with her daughter, son-in-law and four grandchildren. Her husband expired few years back due to illness and her son left her home. Regular conflict with her daughter-in-law was the major reason for son's separation from the family. He stays separately with his wife and children, and does not have any contact with her. This incident has left a deep impact on her life, as in a patriarchal society, having a son and still staying with daughter is perceived as a burden by her.

When she started working in the garden, she used to get around Rs. 2-3 weekly. But over the years her wages increased. Along with wages she also used to get various provisions like housing facility, ration, firewood and provident fund benefits. At the time of retirement she got a lump sum amount of Rs. 3-4 lakhs which consist of provident fund, gratuity and one time retirement pension. She did not get the amount immediately and had to go many times to get the amount after her retirement. With the amount that she received at the time of retirement, she added two rooms to her one room house. She also constructed a ring well as earlier they had to fetch water from neighbour's well. Some amount of money she saved in her bank account, which she uses to buy essentials and for the needs of her grandchildren. Over time her money is almost finished and now she is depended on her daughter and son-in-law to fulfil her needs. She spent her whole life managing responsibilities, taking care of her family, doing household work and working whole year but post-retirement her life changed.

She gets bored as she does not have much work to manage. She spends most of her time now in roaming around the labour lines. She feels blessed to have four grandchildren who give her company and help in reducing her boredom to a certain extent. Two of her grandsons and one grand-daughter go to school whereas one grand-daughter goes to *anganwadi*. She adores her grandchildren and loves to spend time with them. When they go to school and her daughter and son-in-law go to work, she feels time has stopped. She is not used to sitting idle as she always had a busy schedule. She had to get up early in the morning, manage household work and then leave for work. She never got time to rest. These long years of hard work had taken toll on her health and now illness has gripped her. She constantly suffers from back pain and leg pain. She also gets easily tired and feels weak.

Reena has handed over almost all her responsibilities to her daughter and son-in-law after retirement. The household decisions are mostly taken by them. She herself does not speak much on these issues. Even decisions regarding household expenses are taken by them. Sometimes, they seek her opinion on certain things. All her life she had taken enough responsibilities, so she does not feel the need to interfere much. The only responsibility she has now is to take care of her grandchildren when their parents are at work. But she loves this responsibility as they keep her occupied. She gets lonely when she has to stay alone. Earlier she also used to manage household work but her daughter has freed her from it. Her daughter manages most of the household work before going to work. Reena contributes whatever she can to make their life easier but now she does not have much to do. She had done what she could do for her children. Her neighbours and friends perceive that she led a holistic and happy life, as she completed all her responsibilities, and has a loving family who take care of her. But is this the reality?

She is content but there are few things which have gripped her. She feels lonely, she feels frustrated and she feels that she is a burden on her family. She also feels like having her son back and playing with her grandchildren, but she is aware that it might never happen. This saddens her and makes her feel more dependent on her daughter. Financially also she is dependent on her daughter. Reena also failed to avail certain benefits as she is not aware of government schemes, Acts and policies for the welfare of the elderly. She only has a ration card in her name which helps her in getting fixed ration at a subsidized rate. She does not receive widow pension, rather does not even have an iota of an idea about it. She feels if government has made certain schemes for their benefit, they should be made aware of it.

Although she is not neglected by her daughter, but still she is leading a life of dependency. Her needs and other requirements are taken care of by her daughter. Her grandchildren love her. Overall she is aware of her future life which she has to spend in dependency, ill health and solitude.

Role of geriatric social worker

Geriatric social workers help find solutions for older adults and families that address the personal, social, and environmental challenges that come with aging. Geriatric social workers' main priority is maintaining and enhancing the quality of life of elderly clients. This may include developing an understanding not only about the physical complications of aging, but mental health, cultural barriers, and organizational challenges faced by the elderly. They help families by gathering information about the array of services available to them, coordinating care across various health systems, facilitating family support, and providing direct counselling services (e-caring, 2012). Geriatric social workers also help elderly individuals adjust to and cope with the problems they may experience. These professionals help make sure that the needs of their elderly clients are met, each and everyday. Before that they first assess each client in order to determine exactly what their needs are. They also help them with financial issues, medical care, mental disorders, and social problems. It also helps them determine what their clients' abilities and limitations are. The social workers can then work on a plan to help meet the needs of their clients. This usually involves helping clients utilize services that they may not have known about or that they may have found confusing or complicated. For example, a geriatric social worker who finds that a client is struggling financially may help that client either find part-time employment or apply for financial assistance, depending on that client's abilities and limitations.

There are various NGOs working for the welfare of tea plantation society. But in Durrung tea estate, there is no NGO working for the benefits of the labourers. However, there is an urgent need of geriatric social workers who can work with the elderly population of tea plantation sector. Elderly in tea plantation society suffer from various problems like financial issues, neglect, health issues, malnutrition, abuse, etc. so, they need a helping hand to overcome their problems and lead a life of respect, free from wants and dependencies. However, their issues vary and so a geriatric social worker can utilise the principles of case work such as individualisation and self-determination in dealing with individual cases. Social casework is a method of helping people individually through one-to-one relationship. It is a professionalised activity whose focus is to help people in distress who cannot help themselves (Mathew, 1992). Social worker must access the needs and requirements of the elderly and provide them with the required information and help them decide what they want to do. Social worker must respect their decisions. The tea plantation labourers lead a simple life; they have spent all their lives within the garden. So, a social worker while working with them must respect their feelings and opinions.

In Reena's case, a geriatric social worker can use the four components of case work, i.e., person, problem, place and process to organise their thoughts about the client, her situation and required social work intervention (Perlman, 1957). Social worker should assess the client, her strength and weaknesses and look at various dimensions of the client (physical, emotional, psychological, social and economic) that affects the client's situation. Then the social worker should assess the client's problems by interacting with her and by trying to understand the issues faced by her. Social worker should build a good rapport to better understand her problem. The problems faced by Reena are mainly loneliness, feeling burdened upon her daughter and son-in law, financial dependence on her daughter and health issues of back pain, leg pain, weakness and constant tiredness. So, after assessing the problems of the client, social worker should assess how the government and non-governmental organisations can provide benefits to the client. What facilities will prove beneficial to the client can be evaluated. After assessing the person, problem and place, social worker should assess the process of helping the client. Social worker in Reena's case can adopt the counselling method, give information, link clients to resources available and help them access appropriate treatment facilities. By focussing on these four components of case work, social worker can understand the problems of the client and help her deal with it.

Reena had worked whole life and fulfilled all her responsibilities of work sphere and household, but after retirement when she failed to contribute financially or help in household work, she started feeling like a burden on her daughter. In this case, social worker can first try to understand why she thinks so or does her daughter or son-in-law ever made her feel like a burden on them. Social worker must emphasis on her contribution, how she takes care of the grandchildren in absence of their parents and it is a great relief for them to know that their children are safe. Social worker can make her realize her importance in the family, her contribution to the family by being a constant supporter, a guide, a care-taker of the children and a guardian. Reena also feels lonely after her retirement since her family remains busy with their work. She does not blame them because she herself has spent a busy life all these years trying to manage work sphere as well as household work. So, social worker can provide her counselling; spend some time with her sharing her joys and sorrows. Social worker can make her understand that it is inevitable for an elderly to feel loneliness due to reduced connection with friends and relatives or inability to actively participate in community activities. Social worker can encourage her to visit her friends and neighbours, participate in community functions which take place within the community. This may help her to feel less lonely.

At present Reena is also financially dependent on her daughter and son-in-law, so social worker can help her by providing awareness about various financial assistance schemes like widows pension and help her in utilizing it. Reena also do not have BPL card, so social worker must help her in getting a BPL card, which will also help her to access widow pension under Indira Gandhi National Widows Pension scheme. Most of the time widows like Reena fail to utilise benefits of various schemes and services because of lack of awareness, so by providing awareness social worker can help them in getting financial assistance.

Regarding her ill health, social worker can access her health issues by discussing with her and her family members. With consultation with the doctor of garden hospital, make a treatment plan. Social worker can provide her awareness about the health issues, causes and treatment options. Social worker can also assist her in getting health benefits and health pensions which will help her to get free treatment. Social worker can help access the benefits under Atal Amrit Abhiyan scheme under which those under BPL can get health insurance for 437 illnesses. Thus, it can be said that there is an urgent need of geriatric social worker who can work with elderly population of tea plantation society. These labourers remain bounded within the garden. Mostly women labourers suffer from various forms of exploitation, abuse and oppression. The elderly women suffer from neglect, abuse and have to depend on others for day-to-day needs. Therefore, in such a scenario, a geriatric social worker can help them in accessing various resources and lead a life without being dependent on others free from neglect and abuse.

Conclusion

Tea plantation labourers lead a hard life. They have to struggle for their basic needs. Women tea plantation labourers are also significant part of the plantation sector, but they never received due recognition and appreciation. Those women after their retirement further have to live a life depending on others. Due to their isolation and ignorance, they fail to access most of the benefits and schemes. In such a scenario, a geriatric social worker by focusing on the four components of case work can better understand the clients and their problems which will also help to make an intervention plan to resolve their issues. Social worker can help them by providing awareness, help them in accessing various benefits and schemes and provide them emotional support and guidance. Overall, they can help the elderly to lead a life free from neglect, abuse and dependency.

REFERENCES

Bhadra, M., (1985). "Women Workers in Tea Plantations". *Indian Anthropologist, 15*(02), 93-114.

Borah, N., (2013). The rights of women workers in the tea gardens of Assam. *The Clarion: Multidisciplinary International Journal, 2*(2), 128-131.

Chatterjee, S., & Das, R., (1981). Tea-Labour in Assam: Recruitment and Government Policy, 1840-80. *Economic and Political Weekly, 16*(44/46), 1861-1868.

E-Caring, (2012). What does a geriatric social worker do?Retrieved from https://www.healthworkscollective.com/what-does-geriatric-social-worker-do/

Mathew, G., (1992). *An Introduction to Social Case Work.* Bombay: Tata Institute of Social Sciences.

Perera, R. & Holmes, W., (2005). The health and well-being of older people and their families in the tea estates of Sri Lanka. Centre for International Health Burnet Institute. Retrieved from http://silverinnings.in/wp-content/uploads/2016/10/srilanka-sr.citizen-info.pdf

Perlman, H.H., (1957). *Social Casework: A Problem Solving Process.* London: University of Chicago Press.

Start a Geriatric Social Worker. (n.d). Retrieved from https://careersinpsychology.org/become-a-geriatric-social-worker/

12
Scope of Social Work Intervention for Geriatric Cancer with Reference to Rural South Assam Cancer Care Setting

Amit Das

Introduction

Cancer is a major cause of morbidity and mortality in both developing and developed countries (Ferley *et al.,* 2013). Day by day the problem of cancer is growing and having an increasing trend. The studies (Yancik, 1997; Pallis *et al.,* 2010) mentioned that, the incidence of cancer after the age of 65 years has increased 11-fold compared to younger people. Other studies (Neppl-Huber *et al.,* 2012; Znaor *et al.,* 2013; Arnold *et al.,* 2015) found that the median age of cancer diagnosis lies beyond the age of 60 years like the cancers of breast, colon, kidney, myeloma, and prostate. Thus, these shows that elderly cancer is common throughout the world.

As per population census 2011, there were about 104 million elderly persons in India; 53 million females and 51 million males. More than 73 million (71%) elderly people reside in rural areas. In India, more than 12-23 per cent of all cancers occur after the age of 65 years and more than 25 per cent of cancers are diagnosed over the age of 60 years (Agarwal *et al.,* 2002). Advancing age is a risk factor for cancer, with persons over 65 about 60 per cent of new incidence (Berger *et al.,* 2006; Sarkar and Shahi, 2013).

For elderly people, Marcus Tullius Cicero (a Roman politician and lawyer) quoted that—

> "As I give thought to the matter, I find four causes for the apparent misery of the old age: first, it withdraws us from active accomplishments; second, it renders the body less

powerful; third, it deprives us of almost all forms of enjoyments; fourth, it stands not far from death."

From the above quote, it denotes that the human problem increases with increasing age. So, this is important to study the elderly people, their environment, and their health hazards.

Cancer is a disease of aged people and incidence increases with age (Puts *et al.,* 2014). All these cancer epidemiology stated the risk of aged people. Why aged cancer patients are at more risk? The major reasons from several studies are shown below –

(i) Increasing age (Pal *et al.,* 2010; Sarkar and Shahi, 2013; Puts *et al.,* 2014),
(ii) Functional problem (Extermann *et al.,* 1998),
(iii) Co-morbidities (Koroukian *et al.,* 2006),
(iv) Poor prognosis (Kennedy, 1991),
(v) Inadequate social and family support (Kennedy, 1991),
(vi) Socio-economic issues (Hutchins *et al.,* 2000; Wildiers *et al.,* 2013),
(vii) Less possibilities of curative treatment (Hutchins *et al.,* 2000; Wildiers *et al.,* 2013),
(viii) Decreased quality of life (Kennedy, 1991),
(ix) Poor survival status (Kant *et al.,* 1992),
(x) High mortality (Alan *et al.,* 2013).

The other reasons also include poor psychosocial status, low treatment tolerance, incomplete or no treatment, lifestyle habits, and advanced nature of disease.

Methodology

Descriptive study with 699 elderly cancer patients those who were registered at Cachar Cancer Hospital and Research Centre in the year 2014. Study data were collected retrospectively from the Department of Epidemiology and Tumour Registry. Both primary and secondary data were used in this study. The inclusion age criteria was 60 years and above. The data were analyzed through SPSS and the major statistical procedure includes average, percentage, and chi-square test. The confidence interval limits to 95 per cent. The major results are highlighted in tables and graphs.

Results

Demographic and Socio-economic Status: 1736 cancer patients were registered at Cachar Cancer Hospital and Research Centre (CCHRC) in the year 2014. Out of these 699 (40.26%) patients were belonged to age group of 60 years and above.

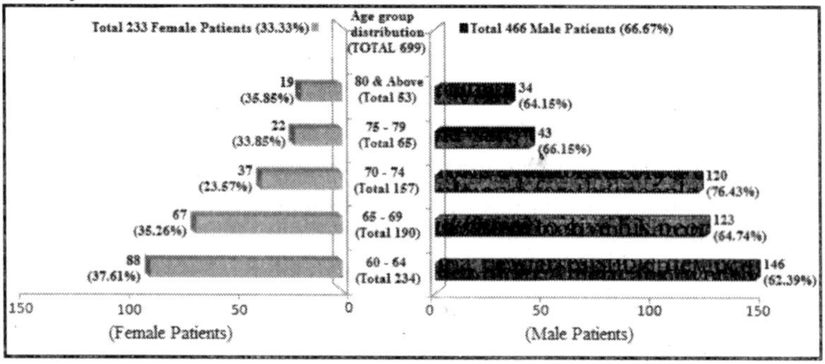

Fig. 12.1: Gender-wise Age Group Distribution of Elderly Patients.

Source: Department of Epidemiology and Tumour Registry, CCHRC.

Fig. 12.1 shows that majority of aged patients were males (66.67%) followed by females (33.33%). The male and female sex ratio was respectively 2:1. Majority of elderly male cancer patients (76.43%) were found in the age group of 70-74 years followed by other age groups.

Majority of 580 elderly patients were registered from Barak Valley (Cachar, Karimganj, and Hailakandi district) which constitute about 82.98 per cent followed by other geographical locations.

Table 12.1: Monthly Family Income of the Elderly Patients

Income Group	No's of Patient	%
Up to Rs. 5000	347	49.64%
5001 – 10000	210	30.04%
10001 - 15000	59	8.44%
15001 - 20000	40	5.72%
20001 - 25000	12	1.72%
25000 & above	31	4.43%
Grand Total	**699**	**100%**

Source: Department of Epidemiology and Tumour Registry, CCHRC.

Table 12.1 represents that 49.64 per cent (347) of elderly patients have family income up to Rs. 5000 per month followed by other income groups.

Tobacco Habits of Aged Cancer Patients

In this study it has been found that 93.78 per cent (437) of males and 88.41 per cent (206) of females were tobacco users. There was significant association at 5 per cent significance level between gender and tobacco habits ($X^2 = 6.197$, df = 1, p = 0.013). Aged males are more likely to have tobacco habits than females. Tobacco habits are a major threat of developing cancer. Figure 12.2 shows that, majority of 61.59 per cent (287) males were both users of tobacco chewing and smoking followed by other habits. Among females, majorities (75.54%) were tobacco chewers. Very less percentage of males (6.22%) and females (11.59%) had no tobacco habits.

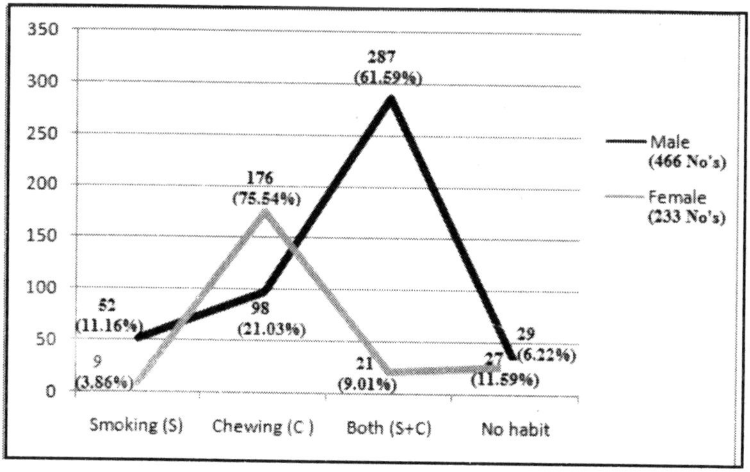

Fig. 12.2: Tobacco Habits of Elderly Cancer Patients.

Clinical Information of Elderly Cancer Patients

Among 466 males, 132 patients (28.33%) were reported with head & neck cancer which was the leading site followed by lung (16.95%), oesophagus (10.73%), and other sites. Among 233 females, 40 patients (17.17%) were reported with gallbladder cancer which was the leading site followed by head & neck (13.73%), lung (12.88%), and other sites. Majority of 78.68 per cent (550) aged patients were microscopically confirmed followed by clinically confirmed cases (16.02%), and radiological confirmed cases (5.29%).

Compliance to Treatment of Geriatric Cancer Cases

Compliance to treatment is an important issue for both patients and clinicians. In this study, it has found that 54.08 per cent (378) of aged patients were remained untreated followed by 29.33 per cent (205) of complete treatment and 16.59 per cent (116) of incomplete treatment. So, overall 321 (45.92%) patients were initiated for their treatment and out of these 144 (44.86%) patients were intended for palliative care/palliation.

Discussion

Cancer is having an increasing trend throughout the world. The studies (Neppl-Huber *et al.,* 2012; Znaor *et al.,* 2013; Arnold *et al.,* 2015) stated that the median age of cancer diagnosis lies beyond the age of 60 years and most frequent cancer sites are breast, colon, kidney, myeloma, and prostate. In this study it has been found that more than 40 per cent of patients were registered belonged to age of 60 and above years and the most frequent site among males was head & neck cancer followed by lung, oesophagus and other sites. Among females, most frequent site was gallbladder cancer followed by head & neck, lung, and other sites.

A study conducted by Parikh and Bakshi (2005) stated that, in India about 10 lakh new cancer incidences are detected every year. As a consequence of demographic changes, a 280 per cent increase in cancer is expected to occur by the year 2025 and further 220 per cent increase in the incidence is expected because of increase in tobacco consumption. So, tobacco use may be a threat of developing new cancer cases in India. In this study, it has seen that more than 93 per cent of males and 88 per cent of females were tobacco users in any form. Aged males are more likely to have tobacco habits than compared to females and it was found statistically significant.

In this study, about 50 per cent of aged patients family income was Rs. 5000 in a month. Cancer treatment needs lots of money to continue treatment and also needs good physical performance status to tolerate treatment. Increasing age may reduce physical performance status of elderly people which is an important indicator for treatment tolerance. But in this study, about 46 per cent of patients were initiated for treatment and out of these about 45 per cent of patients were intended for palliative care. These may be because of elderly patient's poor economic status and poor physical performance status. Elderly cancer patients also have poor survival status and decreased quality of life than compared to younger patients.

Conclusion and Scope of Social Work Intervention:

Geriatric cancer patients' overall compliance of treatment depends on various factors like socio-economic status, lifestyle habits, psychological state, and physical performance status. Because of poor treatment compliance, patients may have poor survival status and quality of life. Social work is a professional service and also having scope for geriatric cancer care. Fig. 12.3 shows the scope of professional social worker in the field of geriatric cancer care –

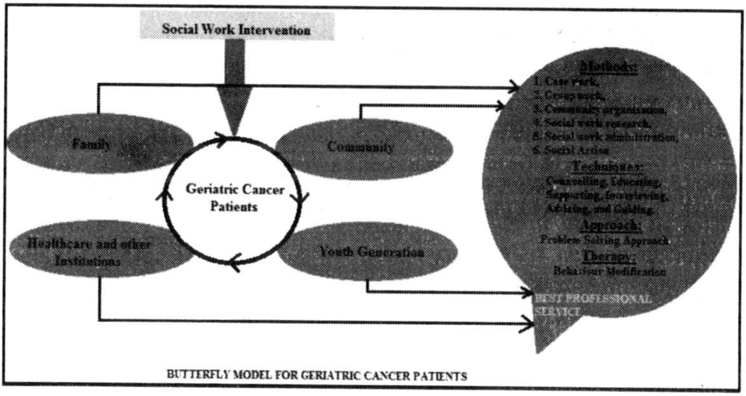

Fig. 12.3: Scope of Professional Social Worker in the Field of Geriatric Cancer Care.

So, the above model suggests that professional social worker have scope to work with geriatric cancer patients in terms of their psychological well-being, physical well-being, functional well-being, behaviour modification, better interpersonal relationships, tobacco cessation, better lifestyle, and overall quality of life. Social workers can also play an active role for better patient's treatment compliance for their best survival.

REFERENCES

Arnold, M., Karim-Kos, H.E., Coebergh, J.W., *et al.,* (2015). "Recent trends in incidence of five common cancers in 26 European countries since 1988: analysis of the European Cancer Observatory". *Eur J Cancer, 51,* 1164-1187.

Agarwal, S. P., Rao, Y. N., & Gupta, S., (2002). "National Cancer Control Program (NCCP)" 1st ed. 2002. '*Fifty years of cancer control in India*' by Rao, Y.N., Gupta, S., & Agarwal, S.P., pp. 41-47.

Alan, O., Gursel, O., Unsal, M., Altin, S., & Kilciksiz, S., (2013). "Oncologic Approach in Geriatric Patients". *Okmeydani Tip Dergisi, 29,* 94-98.

Berger, N.A., Savvides, P., & Koroukian, S.M., (2006). "Cancer in the Elderly". *Transactions of the American Clinical and Climatological Association, 117*, 147-156.

Extermann, M., Overcash, J., Lyman, G.H., *et al.,* (1998). "Comorbidity and functional status are independent in older cancer patients". *J Clin Oncol, 16*, 1582-1587.

Ferlay, J., Soerjomataram, I., Ervik, M., *et al.,* (2013). *Cancer Incidence and Mortality Worldwide.* IARC Cancer Base No. 11. Lyon, France: International Agency for Research on Cancer. http://globocan.iarc.fr (accessed on Feb 27, 2018).

Hutchins, L.F., Unger, J.M., & Crowley, J.J., (2000). "Patients 65 years of age or older in cancer-treatment trials". *The New England Journal of Medicine, 342*, 1531. http://dx.doi.org/10.1056/NEJM200005183422016

Kant, A.K., Glover, C., Horm, J., Schatzkin, A., & Harris T.B., (1992). "Does cancer survival differ for older patients?" *Cancer, 70*, 2734-2740.

Kennedy, B.J. (1991). "Needed: clinical trials for older patients". *J Clin Oncol, 5*, 718-720.

Koroukian, S.M., Murray, P., & Madigan, E., (2006). "Comorbidity, disability, and geriatric syndromes in elderly cancer patients receiving home health care". *Journal of Clinical Oncology, 24*, 2304-2310.

Neppl-Huber, C., Zappa, M., Coebergh, J.W., *et al.,* (2012). "Changes in incidence, survival and mortality of prostate cancer in Europe and the United States in the PSA era: additional diagnoses and avoided deaths". *Ann Oncol, 23*, 1325-1334.

Pal, S.K., Katheria, V. & Hurria, A. (2010). "Evaluating the Older Patient with Cancer: Understanding Frailty and the Geriatric Assessment". *CA: A Cancer Journal for Clinicians, 60*, 120-132.

Pallis, A. G., Fortpied, C., Wedding, U., *et al.,* (2010). "EORTC elderly task force position paper: approach to the older cancer patient". *Eur J Cancer, 46*, 1502-1513.

Parikh, P.M., & Bakshi, A.V., (2005). "Cancer in The Elderly—Get Ready for the 'Epidemic'". *Medicine Update, 166*, 827-831.

Puts, M.T., Tu, H.A., Tourangeau, A., Howell, D., Fitch, M., Springall, E., *et al.* (2014). "Factors influencing adherence to cancer treatment in older adults with cancer: A systematic review". *Ann Oncol, 25*, 564-577.

Sarkar, A., & Shahi, U.P., (2013). "Assessment of Cancer Care in Indian Elderly Cancer Patients: A Single Center Study". *South Asian Journal of Cancer, 2*, 202-208. http://dx.doi.org/10.4103/2278-330X.119904

Wildiers, H., Mauer, M., & Pallis, A., (2013). "End Points and Trial Design in Geriatric Oncology Research: A Joint European Organisation for Research and Treatment of Cancer—Alliance for Clinical Trials in Oncology". *Journal of Clinical Oncology, 31*, 3711-3718. http://dx.doi.org/10.1200/JCO.2013.49.6125

Yancik, R., (1997). "Cancer burden in the aged: an epidemiologic and demographic overview". *Cancer, 80*, 1273-1283.

Znaor, A., van den Hurk, C., Primic-Zakelj, M., *et al.* (2013). "Cancer incidence and mortality patterns in South Eastern Europe in the last decade: gaps persist compared with the rest of Europe". *Eur J Cancer, 49*, 1683-1691.

13
Challenges of Indian Elderly People and Scope of Social Work Intervention

Viveni H. Yeptho, Yhunsille Seb and *Amit Das*

Introduction

Ageing is a natural, inevitable biological phenomenon. The process of ageing had begun much earlier in the developed countries because of the change in fertility and mortality rate. But in the developing countries like India, the scenario is different. In India, the people are considered as aged after attaining the age of 60 and more years. As per Population Census 2011, there were nearly 104 million elderly persons in India with 53 million females and 51 million males. Life expectancies are improved because of declining mortality rate which resulting an increasing proportion of older people in the population (WHO, 1984). The population pyramid of India is showing significant increase in elderly population over a few decades. The country is grappling by the elderly population and having second highest population in the world.

Major problems of elderly people are broadly categorized into two groups (i) problems related to impairment of functional organ, and (ii) mental disturbance caused due to several factors. However, the most prominent problem faced by the elderly people is the abusive behaviour by either their family members or the society. Because of westernization and industrialization, the families are limited by their size, having financial burden, aspirations of children for better way of living, and because of these circumstances most of the elderly people are now helpless. Despite improvements, elderly population in India has to overcome collaborated challenges. Generally, elderly abuse is an intentional negligent act by a family member or any other person that causes harm to an elderly person (Deswal, 2011).

Methodology

The present study followed the descriptive design and all data were collected from the secondary sources like books, journal articles, published and unpublished works on elderly, newspaper, etc. to reflect the current problems and prospects of Indian elderly people.

Demographic Profile of Elderly People in India

As per Population Census 2011 there were nearly 104 million elderly persons in India with 53 million females and 51 million males. As per 2001 Census, the majority of the elderly (75%) were from rural areas and rest 25 per cent were residing in urban areas. Among them, 53 per cent of elderly males were literate followed by 20 per cent of females. As per report of National Sample Survey Organization (2006), about 36 per cent of elderly people were in the labour force which includes 26.9 per cent of self-employed people, 7.4 per cent of casual labour, and 1.5 per cent of regular salaried population. Elderly males were more economically sound than elderly females. As per 2001 Census analysis, 82 per cent of elderly men and 47 per cent of elderly women were still married. More than half of all elderly women were widowed while about 15 per cent of elderly men were widowers. In a study (Alam, 2006) explained that, the ratio of the dependent population to that of the working age population is defined as the dependency ratio and is an important indicator of the economic burden carried by each worker.As per report of National Sample Survey Organization (2004), the old age dependency ratio was higher in rural areas than compared to urban areas. It was also estimated that one-third of the elderly people were living in below poverty line.

Socio-economic Status of Elderly People in India

The modern Indian family structure is changing because of rapid industrialization, globalization, westernization, and urbanization. Due to these changing structures, the elderly people are not given adequate care and attention by their family members. These changes also lead to alienation and isolation of the elderly from their family and society at large. The elderly people are declining their value system, respect, honour, status and authority, which the elderly used to enjoy in traditional societies and hence, elderly people are now in insignificant place in our society (Gupta, 2001). The elderly people in India are also lacking their decision making power and found more common among elderly women (Nandal *et al.,* 1987). A study conducted by Khan and Raikwar (2010) with 320 elderly people in Delhi and found that 89 per cent of elderly people were expecting that their family should take care of them. They found that, only 37 per cent of elderly people were actually taken care of by their families. In their study they also reported that 92 per cent of elderly people felt that they should be included in important household matters and only 26 per cent of elderly people were actually involved. In traditional Indian society, the elder people had more social security because of the informal support systems of family, kinship and community. But the factors of rapid urbanization, industrialization and globalization, the rural families are now migrated towards urban areas for their economic change, better livelihood, and life-style. So, these bring change towards traditional value system and joint families are now converted to nuclear families. As a result, most of the aged people are marginalized in rural India and depends on 'money-order economy' and their intimacy with their children is only from a distance (Kumar, 1999). In urban areas, the cost of living is very high and majority of elderly people are lacking various infrastructures and services in terms of their housing status, earning status, health status, and overall livelihood status. In a study (Sathyanarayana *et al.*, 2012) found that about three-fourths of elderly co-reside either with their spouse and/or children and grandchildren. Elderly people are considered as burden in the family and being sent to various institutions like old age homes for their care. These people had lots of faith on their children but at ending phase of life they were neglected and being sent to other places. That phase is very crucial phase for elderly people to receive their family care and services but most of the elderly people established their new relationships with other institutions and with other neglected elderly people. In some instances, elderly people have their life risks even death by their intimates though their intimates are educated or uneducated. To support this statement, 'Hindustan Times' an Indian newspaper stated that, a 36-year-old assistant professor was arrested for allegedly killing his 64-year-old mother by pushing her off the terrace of their residential building in the city. Initially, the family had claimed that elderly lady fell off the terrace after losing her balance as she was suffering from some brain disease. However, police changed the direction of the investigation on receipt of an unknown application. "After receiving the application, police checked CCTVs installed in the apartment and the recording clearly suggested that assistant professor was with deceased when she fell off the terrace". Police said the assistant professor initially denied the allegation against him, but later "confessed" to his involvement in the crime. So, this reflects that elderly people are also victimized with crimes. In India, elderly people are also found as beggars in some holy places, even in cities, railway stations, and bus stations for their livelihood. In rural areas, families suffer from economic crises because their occupations do not produce income. Inadequate income is a major problem of the elderly in India (Siva Raju, 2002) It is generally believed that the elderly people are burden for their family and as well as nation because they do not contribute to the national income. But in a study (Bhagat and Unisa, 2006) stated that in India, 40 per cent of the elderly who are 60 and above years are working.

Psychosocial and Health Issues of Indian Elderly

Psychosocial and health issues are one more threat to Indian elderly people. In this context, Boralingaiah *et al.* (2012) conducted a study on psychosocial issues among 526 elderly people and found that elderly men are more functional compared to elderly women. Anxiety and insomnia were found in 3.4 per cent of the aged (males 2.4% and females 4.1%) followed by somatic symptoms 2.9 per cent, social dysfunction 1.5 per cent and severe depression 1.1 per cent. All psychological distress was found more among elderly women. The prevalence of mental illnesses was found to be significantly higher for age more than 75 years. The physiological decline refers to the decline in the normal functioning of the body resulting in poor mobility, vision, hearing, indigestion, inability to eat, memory loss and various chronic health problems. In India, the elderly people suffer from dual medical problems, i.e., both communicable as well as non-communicable diseases. In India, the life expectancy is also increased. This increased life expectancy brought several health related hazards like heart disease, locomotors and visual disability, cancer, diabetics, etc.

Addressing elderly abuse have used the definition adopted by the World Health Organization, i.e., a single or repeated act or lack of appropriate action occurring within any relationship where there is an expectation of trust, which causes harm or distress to an older person (WHO, 2002). Elderly abuse is a complex phenomenon that results from several different causes, and that often has roots in multiple factors (Sekher and Sebastian, 2011). Some of the factors are mentioned below –

(a) **Physical Abuse:** defined as bodily injury, physical pain, or impairment,
(b) **Verbal or Psychological Abuse:** defined as pain, or distress through verbal or non-verbal acts,
(c) **Financial abuse:** elderly crisis situation because of their property, finance, or assets.
(d) **Neglect:** both direct and indirect neglect. Direct neglect refers to older people being left alone, isolated, or forgotten. Indirect

neglect refers to withholding of items that are necessary for daily living, such as food and medicine.

Elderly abuse is also seen in terms of taking advantage of their physical weakness by their caretaker like their servants or maids. In India, many metropolitan cities recorded several cases where elderly people have killed or injured them severely for several reasons. Women become victim of rape and physical assault even at older ages. One of the case evident in the data showed an 81 year old woman was raped by her 22 years old servant (*Times of India*). So, the elderly mostly women elderly people are victimized with crime against elderly people in India.

Elderly Care Initiatives taken by Indian Government

Indian Constitution has certain articles to protect these vulnerable sections of our society. Some of the articles are mentioned below –

(a) **Article 41 of Indian Constitution:** According to Article 41 of the constitution of India, "the state shall, within the limits of its economic capacity and development, make effective provision for securing the right to work, to education and to public assistance in cases of unemployment, old age, sickness and disablement and in other cases of undeserved want."

(b) **Article 47 of Indian Constitution:** Article 47 of the constitution of India provides that the state shall regard the raising of the level of nutrition and the standard of living of its people and improvement of public health as among its primary duties.

Apart from this, the Indian Government created several legislative measures and policy framework for the welfare of the elderly people in India. Some of these measures and policies are given below –

(a) **Maintenance and Welfare of Parents and Senior Citizens Act, 2007:** It was enacted 31st December, 2007, to ensure need based maintenance for parents and senior citizens and their welfare. Section 19 of the Maintenance and Welfare of Parents and Senior Citizens Act, 2007 envisages provision of at least one old age home for indigent senior citizens with a capacity of 150 persons in every district of the country.

(b) **National Policy for Older Persons (NPOP):** The National Policy on Older Persons was announced by the Central Government of India in the year 1999 to reaffirm the commitment to ensure the well-being of the older persons. It was a step to promote the health, safety, social security and well-being of elderly in India. This policy enables and supports voluntary and non-governmental organizations to supplement the care provided by the family and provide care and protection to vulnerable elderly people.

(c) **National Council for Older Persons (NCOP):** It was constituted in the year 1999 under the chairpersonship of the Ministry of Social Justice and Empowerment to advise the Government on policies and programmes for older persons, suggest measures to enhance the quality of inter-generational relationships, work as a nodal point at the national level for redressing the grievances of elderly people, etc.

Indian Government also having other policies for these elderly people like Integrated Programme for Older Persons (IPOP), National Old Age Pension (NOAP) Scheme-1994, National Programme for Health Care of Elderly (NPHCE), National Policy on Senior Citizens 2011, etc.

Conclusion and Scope of Social Work Intervention

In conclusion, it has been found that elderly people in India having socio-economic issues, psychological issues, health issues, issues related to crime, etc. Indian Government is continuously working for the welfare of this section through several socio-economic policies. But till in India, the elderly people are being neglected and discriminated on the ground of their advancing age. So, in this respect if professional bodies like social worker can be involved directly than there may be reduction of elderly problems in India. Fig. 13.1 shows the scope of social work intervention.

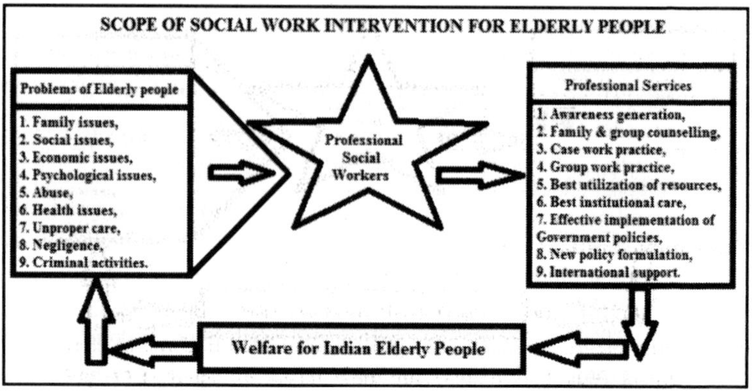

Fig. 13.1: Scope for Social Work Intervention for Elderly People.

Fig. 13.1 states that social work intervention can bring welfare to the elderly people of Indian society through community awareness and sensitization programmes, through counselling and professional guidance, through application of primary social work methods of case work and group work practice, through proper implementation of government policies and framing new policies, and also be able to support elderly people and elderly care institutions through linking them with international agencies.

REFERENCES

Alam, M., (2006). *Ageing in India: Socio-Economic and Health Dimensions.* Academic Foundation, New Delhi.

Bhagat, B.R., & Unisa, S., (2006). "Ageing and dependency in India—A new measurement". *Asian Population Studies, 2*(2), 201-214.

Boralingaiah, P., Bettappa, P., & Kashyap, S., (2012). "Prevalence of psycho-social problems among elderly in urban population of Mysore city, Karnataka, India". *Indian J Psychol Med, 34*(4), 360–364.

Census of India, (2001). Available at www.censusindia.net

Deswal, V.P.S., (2011). "Elder abuse: problems and preventive measures". *Helpage india-research & development journal, 17*(3).

Gupta, N., (2001). *Successful Aging and its determinants: A Study of Elderly in Kolkata.* Tata Institute of Social Sciences, Mumbai.

https://timesofindia.indiatimes.com/city/delhi/Verdict-on-rape-and-murder-of-81-year-old-on-August-6/articleshow/53291526.cms

Khan, A.M., & Raikwar, M., (2010). "Relationship between expectations, life satisfaction and diseases amongst elderly from different social groups". *Indian Journal of Gerontology, 24*(3), 379 - 394.

Kumar, V.S., (1999). *Quality of Life and Social Security for the Elderly in Rural India.* Council for Social Development, Hyderabad.

Nandal, D.S., Dhatri R.S., & Kadian, R.S., (1987). "Ageing problems in the structural context", in M.L. Sharma and T.M. Dak (eds.) *Ageing in India: Challenge for the Society.* pp. 106-16. Ajanta Publications, New Delhi.

National Sample Survey Organization, (2004). available at: http://mospi.gov.in/nsso_4aug2008/web/nsso /sdrd/ design/design_est_60.pdf.

National Sample Survey Organization, (2006). available at: http://mospi.gov.in/nsso_4aug2008/web/nsso / sdrd/design/design_est_62.pdf.

Sathyanarayana, K.M., Kumar, S., & James, K.S., (2012). *Living Arrangements of Elderly in India: Policy and Programmatic Implications.* BKPAI Working Paper, United Nations Population Fund, India.

Sekher, T. V., & Sebastian, D., (2011). "Extent and nature of elder abuse in Indian families: A study in Kerala". *Helpage India-research & development journal,* 17 (3).

Siva Raju, S., (2002). "Meeting the needs of the poor and excluded in India, situation and voices, the older poor and excluded in South Africa and India", UNFPA. *Population and Development Strategies, 2*, 93-110.

World Health Organization, (2002). *Missing Voices: Views of Older Persons on Elder Abuse*. World Health Organisation/International Network for the Prevention of Elder Abuse, Geneva.

World Health Organization, (1984). *Use of Epidemiology in the Study of the Elderly: Report of a WHO scientific group on the epidemiology of ageing*. WHO Technical Report Series No. 706. WHO, Geneva.

www.hindustantimes.com/india-news/rajkot-professor-kills-ailing-mother-by-throwing-her-off-terrace-caught-on-cctv/storyLRNea5938y K8hfce45q UTO.html

14

Elderly: Their Problems and Legislative Initiatives: Exploring Areas of Social Work Intervention

Sukumar Pal, Debotosh Sinha and *Sudipta Biswas*

Conceptual Understanding

Aging is a natural process. It occurs in every human life cycle. Generally, it is a stage at which a person's functional capacity of organs of the human life declines. It's a stage at which he/she declines not only biological aspects but also psycho-social health of self. It makes the person gradually dependent on others and makes the person socially vulnerable. The process of aging however could be best understood at four levels, such as biological aging in which refers to anatomical and psychological changes that occurs with age as the capacity to produce it; psychological aging, which refers to changes in the central nervous system as well as sensory and perceptual organs. It also refers to general decline in mental capabilities that accompany old age; sociological aging referring to the changes in the status and role of elderly person. The problem of aging as it seems that product of industrialization and psycho-social aging—refers to the feeling of loneliness resulting from their disengagement from active role in social and economic life

Demographic Profile of Elderly

UNESCO report shows a steady increase of elderly population observed since 1950 for both developing and developed countries and by 2015 AD the world would witness a 'Geriatric Boom' (Luthra, 1991). Growth of elderly person in India is higher than general population. During 1951-61, it was 21.6 per cent for general population whereas it was 23.9 per cent for elderly population. At present, the same was 17.7 per cent for general population and 35.5 per cent for elderly population (*GOI, Ministry of Statistics and Programme Implementation*, 2016).

In India, the population of elderly has constantly been increasing. In 1951, the population of 60 + in total population was 5.5 per cent which increased to nearly 6 per cent in 1971 and almost 7 per cent in 2001. In absolute terms, the magnitude of such population has increased from nearly 2 crores in 1951 to 7.2 crore in 2001. According to a news covered by Press Trust of India (PTI) on April 22, 2016, number of elderly populations has increased from 7.66 crore (5.6% of population) in 2001 to 10.38 crore (8.6% of population) in 2011. This, of course, can be explained for a result of the success of better health standard and longer life expectancy for our citizens.

Origin of the Problem

Traditionally, the problem of elderly was taken care of by the joint family but breakdown of the family and changes in traditional norms and values of society have made them more vulnerable. They are sometimes abused by their own family members who are supposed to take care of their parents or elder persons. The problem of elderly was less in the joint family because feeling of insecurity was absent; but breakdown of joint family system has aggravated the problem of elderly. In many cases, young family members consider them as burden and they become subject to ill-treatment. As a result, they suffer emotional problem, leading to frustration and helplessness.

They do face economic and health problem as their physique does not permit them to work and earn their living. They have to depend on wards. On the other hand, their medical expenses go high with increase of age. Their housing problem is on the rise because of urban culture where flat system is the rule of the day. In such a small space they do not get proper accommodation and congenial atmosphere to live freely. People love to live in a nuclear family and as a result of this significant number of Old Age Homes are coming into the scene.

Social problem arises due to physical and economic disabilities; aged persons lose their importance in the family, which they used to enjoy during their active life. They cannot play effective role in the community also as a result of which their social status decreases. This gives them the sense of losing everything and makes them frustrated. It forces them to lose self-esteem and become somewhat isolated, which ultimately brings mental agony, frustration and helplessness.

Legal Safeguards

We observe some safeguards in our Constitution, for instance, Article 41 of the Constitution provides effective provision for securing right to work, to education and to public assistance in cases of employment, old age, sickness and disablement, and in other cases of undeserved want (*Sign the Petition*, n.d.). The statutory provision for maintenance of parents under Hindu Personal Law is contained in Section 20 of *The Hindu Adoption and Maintenance Act, 1956* (Parida, 2020). This is the first statutory law in the country which makes the offspring of the elderly parents accountable to take care of their parents. Prior to 1973, there was no provision for maintenance of parents under the CrPC (Parida, 2020). In that year, Sec.125 was introduced for the first time in Cr.PC which clearly spells out that parents need to establish that the other party has sufficient means and neglected or refused to maintain them, i.e., the parent, who are unable to maintain themselves. This is applicable to any person belonging to any religion and community (Parida, 2020). It also mentions that apart from sons, daughters, including married daughters, also have an obligation to maintain their parents. But none of the above-mentioned Acts bestow any special attention on the aged people or the senior citizens, who have hitherto been neglected.

Hence, a new legislation called the Maintenance and Welfare of Parents and Senior Citizens Act, 2007was passed (Sharma, 2012). The Act sought to redress this grievance with an emphasis and focus on the senior citizens. The Act received President's assent on 29th December, 2007. The Act came into force in State of Maharashtra on 27th August, 2008. The Act has come into force, as on January 12th, 2009, in 19 states and 6 Union Territories to address the problem of elderly.

The basic features of this Act are:

i. It is now the duty and legal obligation for children and heirs to provide maintenance to their parents. The state government may also set up one or more maintenance tribunals at sub-division level to decide upon the order for maintenance. The maximum maintenance allowance shall be prescribed by the State government, and shall not exceed Rs. 10,000 per month (*The Maintenance and Welfare of Parents and Senior Citizens Bill, 2007— Legislative Brief*, n.d.-a).

ii. The tribunal may even order for interim maintenance while the application is pending which needs to be paid by children or relatives. (*State and The Elderly—SKH*, n.d.). The application needs to be disposed of within 90 days, as practicable.

iii. The maintenance allowance is liable to be paid within 30 days of the order, otherwise, a simple interest payment of 5 to 18 per cent of the monthly allowance from the date of the application be paid (The Maintenance and Welfare of Parent and Senior Citizen Act, 2007).
iv. The State Government may establish one appellate tribunal per district to be presided over by an officer not below the rank of District Magistrate. The appellate tribunal may issue the written order within one month of the appeal (The Maintenance and Welfare of Parent and Senior Citizen Act, 2007).
v. The tribunal may issue a warrant for collection of maintenance fee within three months of the due date if there is any failure to comply with. If the accused fail to pay fees, he may be sent to prison for a month or until payment (The Maintenance and Welfare of Parent and Senior Citizen Act, 2007).
vi. Abandonment of a senior citizen may invite an imprisonment of up to three months or fine of up to Rs. 5,000, or both (*New Indian Express*, 2019). The transfer of property (as gift or otherwise) from a senior citizen to a transferee may be declared by the tribunal to be null and void if the transfer was made under the condition of maintenance and the transferee neglects the agreement. If any senior citizen is unable to enforce his/her rights, a registered voluntary organization may take action on behalf of him/her. (*The Maintenance and Welfare of Parents and Senior Citizens Bill, 2007—Legislative Brief*, n.d.).
vii. The State government can now set up one old age home per district with a minimum capacity of 150 senior citizens per home. Otherwise, the state government may also adopt a scheme for the management of such homes. The standards and services to be provided (including those required for medical care and entertainment of residents of these old age homes) should be specified in the scheme (*The Maintenance and Welfare of Parents and Senior Citizens Bill, 2007—Legislative Brief, n.d.*).

Government Programme or Effort for Senior Citizens

As per the National Policy on Older Persons, 1999, Ministry of Social Justice & Empowerment is the nodal Ministry who looks after the welfare of the senior citizens. The policy recognizes a person as a senior citizen if s/he attains the age of 60 years. This policy prescribes for setting up a pension fund, construction of old age home, establishment of resource centre and re-employment bureau, concession of rail and air fares for travel, enacting legislation for their compulsory care, etc. The Ministry of Social Justice and Empowerment in pursuance of the National Policy for Older Persons (NPOP), constituted National Council for Elder Person (NCOP) in 1999 which was then renamed in 2012 as National Council of Senior Citizens (NCSrC) for receiving suggestion, complaint and grievances from individual older person.

The government policy promotes a prompt settlement of pensions, PF, gratuity in order to save superannuated person. A host of other programmes are there such as *Annapurna Yojana* and *Antyodaya Yojana* meant for the elderly people. Under the *Antyodaya Scheme*, the Below Poverty Line families having older persons are provided food grains at the rate of 35 kgs per family per month are issued @ Rs. 3 per kg for rice and Rs. 2 per kg for wheat provides for. While Annapurna Yojana 10 kg of food grains per beneficiary per month given free of cost to those senior citizens. (*Vikaspedia Domains*, n.d.). Central government declared rebate in income tax for elderly people. Assistance is provided to Voluntary Organisations who establish and maintain Old Age Homes, Day Care Centres, and Mobile Medicare Units and provide non-institutional services to older persons. Ministry of Finance have declared higher rates of interest on saving schemes for senior citizens. Indian Railways provide 30 per cent fare concession in all Mail/Express including Rajdhani/ Shatabadi/Jan Shatabadi trains to senior citizens. Indira Gandhi National Old Age Pension Scheme (IGNOAPS), Jan Arogya, Concession as per Ministry of Road Transport policy, Old Age Homes and Day Care Centres, National Programme for Health Care of Elderly (NPHCE), wheelchairs for use of older persons at all junctions and other important stations, etc. are some of the helpful initiatives of the government for the well-being of the older persons.

Cases Study and Its Analysis

Despite the above provisions and legislative action as initiated by Government of India, the plight of elderly continue to be worst. An analysis of their problems reveals the major areas such as economic deprivation and insecurity, restricted mobility due to ill-health physical insecurity, reduction in dignity and self-esteem, loneliness due to rejection, lack of meaningful occupation and leisure activities, lack of protective supportive shelter (National Commission for Women, n.d).

Plight of some elderly people are narrated below based on the news from secondary sources:

Case No. 1: J.S. Bhatia had always dreamt for a happy retired life with his children. Unfortunately, his dreams did not come true. He was abused, refused food and finally abandoned by his son and daughter-in-law. Now, his destination is an old age home in New Delhi. Actually, Bhatia is not the only one to have suffered abuse, mental agony and abandonment. Around 62 per cent elders from Delhi itself and 54 per cent elders from Kolkata reported emotional abuse (helpageindia). The major reasons behind non-disclosure of abuse are "maintaining confidentially of the family matter" in 33 per cent cases followed by "fear of retaliation" in 39 per cent cases. Many others suffered and tolerated the abuse by suppressing the fact as they "did not know how to deal with the problem". 92 per cent of the elderly did not register any type of complaint against the abuser (helpageindia). The most common forms of abuse experienced by the elderly were 'disrespect' (34%), followed by 'verbal abuse' (37%) and 'physical abuse' including beating/slapping (34%) (helpageindia). The survey report clearly indicates that many such cases go unreported every year. As against Bhatia, who chose to come out in the open, as many as 70 per cent of the respondents confessed that they were abused but they did not report the matter (*Hindustan Times*, 2013).

Case No. 2: Aarati Dhar (2013) reported in *The Hindu*, April 28, 2013 that Savitri Sharma lives in Birla Ashram, Varanasi. Despite having four daughters and one son in Rajasthan, she had to take resort to the Ashram. Savitri narrated her story, "Daughters are married and cannot keep me as their husbands disagree to take responsibility. My only son has been living with his in-laws for the past 30 years and he is least bothers about me. I spent some years with my brother-in-law and sister-in-law as long as they were live. None of my daughters took me to her house. I realized that their economic condition would make them feel overburdened. Then I decided to spend the rest of my life in Varanasi" (Dhar, 2013). Her daughter is connected over telephone and sometimes calls her to come back and stay with them, but her conscience does not permit to go back. She also narrated her present situation, "We do get some government relief of Rs. 300 per month which is very irregular. There are no doctors in the ashram or vicinity and private treatment is difficult to afford" (Dhar, 2013).

Case No. 3: A report in *The Hindu* (April 28, 2013) reported that a few kilometers away in Sarnath there is an old age home which is meant for widows. It is a government run old-age home which houses close to 60 elderly women. Surprisingly, all inmates are not widow there. Some are there because their families cannot support them. Due to their age, they are unable to work. They feel themselves as a burden on the society and decide to resort to this old-age home. "Some of them even work for making garlands and necklaces or incense stick and send money back home to support their families financially", explained Anita Pal, In-Charge of Old Age Home (Dhar, 2013).

Discussion and Conclusion in view of Geriatric Social Work

The problems of elderly as observed are manifold such as abuse, lack of care and management, poor financial condition. A majority in the elderly are in the age group of 60 – 69 (48%). Females (65%) outnumbered the males (35%). Majority of the elderly are from rural background (71%). The magnitude of elder abuse in a study found to be 35.2 per cent (Asappa *et al.,* 2016). Regarding the type of elder abuse, majority of the residents experienced verbal abuse (70%) followed by physical abuse (13%). Daughter-in-law was involved in majority of the cases of elder abuse (45.9%), followed by their son (24.3%) (Asappa *et al.,* 2016). "What adds to their misery is the fact that government intervention is inadequate. What is required is an attitudinal change, which ensures that a woman is allowed to lead a normal dignified life in her own household even after her husband dies and is not forced to lead a sub-human life in places such as Vrindavan and Kashi", says social scientist Dr. Ranjana Kumari, Director of the Centre for Social Research in New Delhi. It is a measure of the indignity they suffered back home, hardly any of the women spoken to wanted to be rehabilitated in their native surroundings and instead preferred the incognito status in Vrindavan (*Frontline*, Vol. 23, 2006).

Supportive measures that may require for facilitating meaningful participation of elderly be given focus of attention as some are doing some productive work in different old age homes, such as making garlands and necklaces or incense stick. It is necessary to evaluate the effectiveness and subsequently to take up role of NGOs to engage the able and interested elderly for productive work by creating a good environment.

Geriatric social work practice has to integrate all the above facts for a systematic understanding and planning for elderly care. Some implications for geriatric social work practice are discussed below:

i. *Assessment of the Problem*: The first step should be planning for intervention with elderly, who require care, is to assess the problem. An assessment of the percentage of disabled elderly living in a community and their living arrangements has to be made at the outset. Housing is a key factor for quality of life for elderly. Safe, secure, comfortable and affordable housing is associated with life expectancy (Desai & Raju, 2000). The problem of assessment requires a closer look at type and extent of disability (Bali, 1996), type of support required and day to day care required.

ii. *Assessment of Resources available to Older Persons*: It includes a realistic assessment of different types of resources available for older person that may help in independent living in the community and avoiding institutionalisation. These include economic resources, care of disorders and ensure psychological care.

iii. *Planning for Care:* Against this background of the problem posed and available resources, decision is required regarding how and where care would be provided. It needs following areas of attention:

iv. *Care at home*: It has been the experience of the developed countries that institutionalization is not always the right answer. Most countries are shifting their policies more towards encouraging informal and family care (Badlock & Evers, 1994).

v. *Need Assessment for Partial Institutionalization*: Short term institutionalization of the care recipient is an option to be considered. Utilizing the services of day centres and day care provisions should be assessed.

vi. *Requirements for Tailor-made versus Standardized Services*: Social workers need to evaluate each person's requirements and prepare and individualized programme as far as possible. Singh (1996) aptly points out, there are common human needs of the elderly, yet marked individual variations. Hence, promotion of preventive services has to be individualised and (*Hindustan Times* 2013, June 14).70 per cent elderly abuse cases not reported..https://www.hindustantimes.com/delhi/70-elderly-abuse-cases-not-reported/story-a0v9wEq9XSiBZEIje2r0fL.htmlneed to be uniform for everyone.

vii. *Care related issues*: Many researchers have started focussing physical and psychological impact of long-term care giving on the carers (Jamuna, 1996, Rajkumar *et al.,* 1996). Concern for the use of career should be an integral part of social work with older person. Professionals should identify resources, assess quality care, option, and alternatives available to the career with regard to care giving, counselling the carer to resolve conflicts (Jamuna, 1996). Medical and psychological help to the carers to prevent burnout.

viii. *Regular health care and basic necessities of life*: It should be taken care of by integrating the government benefits such as mobile health care, day care centres at community level for community based rehabilitation with greater attention on recreational activities.

ix. Integrated approach and providing a host of other supportive measures for the welfare of elderly is necessary (Beland & Arweller, 1996).

Concluding Remarks

In geriatric social work is a complex issue and it needs balance the family well-being against the individual well-being (Prakash, 1995). Many elder people are not willing to stay in Old Age Home. Their behaviour may be too dysfunctional for family members to manage. Cognitive decline may be pronounced, or multiple physical disorders too complicated for the career to cope with. The family life of the client may be getting disrupted due to the behaviour of the client as well as the burden on the carer. In such situation, the case worker may advise them for institutionalization in the interest of family well-being. A humanistic solution to such situations one should work out which could be both practical and culturally acceptable in such cases. There are several such emerging issues that will confront the professionals working in the field of gerontology. Besides, a range of supportive services are required to manage elderly care. Environmental modification theory can be applied as treatment approach that can enable caregivers to manage daily care and maintain individual dementia at home.

REFERENCES

Asappa *et al.*, (2016). "Bringing elder abuse out of the shadows: a study from the old age homes of Davangere district, Karnataka, India". *Int J Community Med Public Health*. 2016 June: *3*(6):1617-1622

Aarati Dharm, (2013). *The Hindustan Times*, June 15, 2013.

Badlock and Evers, (1994). "Innovation and Care of the Elderly: The Frontline of Change for Social Welfare Services". *Aging International* (Li): 28-32.

Beland and Arweller, (1996). "A Frame of Reference for Elaborating Policies of Long-Term Care". *Canadian Journal of Aging, 15* (4): 532-648

Desai &Raju, (2001). *Gerontological Social Work in India*. Delhi, B.R. Publishing Corporation.

Dhar, A., (2013, April 28). "A tale of two cities—Vrindavan and Varanasi". *The Hindu*. https://www.thehindu.com/news/national/other-states/a-tale-of-two-cities-vrindavan-and-varanasi/article4663717.ece

Frontline (Vol. 23) 2006. http://www.frontline.in/static/html/fl2316/stories/20060825001305100.htm

Government of India, Ministry of Statistics and Programme Implementation (2016), *Elderly in India*, http://mospi.nic.in/sites/default/files/publication_reports/ElderlyinIndia_2016.pdf

Helpageindia, (n.d.). *Elder Abuse India 2010 Report,* p. 7. Retrieved from helpageindia: https://www.helpageindia.org/pdf/surveysnreports/elderabuseindia2010.pdf

Hindustan Times, (2013, June 14). *70 per cent elderly abuse cases not reported..* https://www.hindustantimes.com/delhi/70-elderly-abuse-cases-not-reported/story-a0v9wEq9XSiBZEIje2r0fL.html

Jamuna, 1996, Rajkumar *et al.,* (1996) in edited book Desai and Raju, *Gerontological Social Work in India*, pp. 243-249.

MoSJEGoI. (n.d.). Retrieved from Ministry of Social Justice and Empowerment, Government of India.: https://socialjustice.nic.in/oldageact.php

National Commission For Women (n.d) *Status of Widows of Vrindavan and Varanasi:A Comparative Study*, http://griefandrenewal.com/widows_study.htm

National Policy on Older Persons on January 13, 1999.

New Indian Express. (2019, December 04). New bill lets senior citizens claim up to Rs 10K per month from children. Retrieved from newindianexpress: http://cms.newindianexpress.com/explainers/2019/dec/04/new-bill-lets-senior-citizens-claim-up-to-rs-10k-per-month-from-children-2071448.html

Parida, D.N., (2020). "Rights of the elderly people: A legal framework analysis". *International Journal of Law*, *6*(1), 249-255.

PIB Delhi. (2021, August 10). Ministry of Social Justice & Empowerment National Council of Senior Citizen. Retrieved from PIB : https://pib.gov.in/PressReleaseIframePage.aspx?PRID=1744553

Prakash, I.J., (1995). "Psychosocial Situation of the elderly: Some emerging Issues", *Indian Journal of Social Psychiatry, 1*(1), 26-29.

Press Trust of India (PTI), April 22, 2016.

Sec. 125 of the Code of Criminal Procedure in 1973.

Shodhganga.inflibnet.ac.in/bitstream/10603/54462/13/13_chapter%207.pdf

Sign the Petition. (n.d.). Retrieved August 23, 2021, from https://www.change.org/p/prime-minister-of-india-save-senior-citizens-and-now-time-to-protect-their-financial-and-health-needs-in-india

Singh, R.R., (1996). "Family Change, elder care needs and social policy". In Vinod Kumar (Edited), *Aging: Indian Perspective and Global Scenario*, (12-19), New Delhi, All India Institute of Medical Sciences.

State and The Elderly—SKH. (n.d.). Retrieved August 23, 2021, from https://www.socialworkfootprints.org/special-articles/state-and-the-elderly

The Hindu Adoption and Maintenance Act, 1956.

The Maintenance and Welfare of Parents and Senior Citizens Bill, 2007—Legislative Brief. (n.d.-a). Retrieved August 23, 2021, from http://www.commonlii.org/in/other/INPRSLS/tmawopascb2007lb665/

The Maintenance and Welfare of Parent and Senior Citizen Act, 2007.(n.d.). The maintenance and welfare of parent and senior citizen Act, 2007. Retrieved from indiacode: https://www.indiacode.nic.in/bitstream/123456789/8865/1/200756senior_citizenact.pdf

Vikaspedia Domains, (n.d.). Retrieved August 23, 2021, from https://vikaspedia.in/social-welfare/senior-citizens-welfare/concessions-and-facilities-given-to-senior-citizens

15

Health Care Services Provided to Elderly

A Case Study of Jeevan Deep Senior Citizen's Home, Cachar

Sabina Begam Ahmed

Introduction

Ageing is a universal process. Increasing proportion of ageing population is a global phenomenon and it has hit Indian shores as well. The population of elderly is consistently increasing and there is a need to focus on their health problems and needs. The reduction in fertility level, reinforced by steady increase in the life expectancy has produced fundamental changes in the age structure of the aging population. Elderly or old age consists of ages nearing or surpassing the average life span of human beings. The period of old age cannot be defined exactly because it does not carry same meaning in all societies. Govt of India adopted "National Policy on Older Persons" in January, 1999. The policy defines 'senior citizens' or 'elderly' as a person who is of age 60 years or above. According to Population Census 2011, there are nearly 104 million elderly persons (aged 60 years or above) in India. Generally, health means the state of being free from illness or injury. The United Nations World Health Organisation (March, 2018) has defined heath as "A state of complete physical, mental and social well-being and not merely the absence of disease or infirmity". Physical health can be defined as a state of well-being in when all internal and external body parts, organs, tissues and cells can function properly, as they are supposed to function. Thus, physical health is a state of physical well-being in which a person is physically fit to perform their daily activities without restrictions. On the other hand, mental health refers to person's emotional, social and psychological well-being. Mental health is as important as physical heath to a full active lifestyle. Health status is an important factor that decides the quality of life of an individual. Ageing is the natural stage of human life, it brings with it innumerable problems for the people who have grown old.

Review of Literature

Few literature related to the study are reviewed in the following paragraphs- A study on the issues and challenges of older women in old age homes by Umadevi, L. & Kiran, V.K., 2015. The study reveals that most of respondents were having average physical health condition. The results of study further reveal that they have less satisfaction with life; they display negative emotions like depression, loneliness.

The study describes the various aspects of the life of elderly people residing in an old age home of Delhi by Lalon, Y., 2014. The study reflects that residents of old age home are from different caste and religion and even spoke different languages as well in some cases. Most of the women in old age home spent their whole lives in doing household works and had no income for their livelihood which forced them to depend on their family and due to this reason; the female residents were more in numbers in old age home as compared to their male. The study reveals that those old persons who live in old age homes is more under stress than those who live with their family members.

An empirical work applied to know the health issues of older people by Nesa, M.A. *et al.*, 2013. The study reveals that economically backward older persons in rural areas face very difficult situation to maintain their basic needs. Several older persons have solely homestead land however no agricultural land. The health standing of older population isn't thus sensible and that they lack access to basic health facilities. About 80 per cent of the elderly population suffered from health problems and almost every one suffered from at least one disease during three months prior to the survey. The average duration of suffering from diseases ranged from 3 years to 9 years. The vibration analysis shows that age, sex, access to treatment and financial gain is related to the health issues of the older population.

The empirical study were conducted in the Karnataka state of India, Ramesh, 2013 and randomly selected some Old age home in the Karnataka. The main focus of the study were the health problems, health status, the functional abilities, the risk factors, sickness and the quality of life affecting of the elderly people those are staying in government and non-government old age home in Karnataka. The total 120 samples were collected in 24 different government and non-government old age homes in Mysore and Mandya district of Karnataka. So, the study found that the maximum inmates are economically dependents, should promote more govt old age home for the elderly people, and the inmates are suffering from physiological and psychological problems so, the more recreational facilities should be provided to encourage them and the government should promote and provide free medical treatment and surgeries free of cost.

An empirical work carried out in Pondicherry to understand the major health problems faced by the elderly from 213 elderly population of aged 60 and above by Balamurugan, J. & Ramathirtham, G., 2012. Findings reveal that majority of the elderly, both male and female, are unhealthy. The most common health problems aged people face include eye sight, hearing, joint pains, nervous disorders, weakness, heart complaints, asthma, tuberculosis, skin diseases, urinary problems and others. More health problems were reported by women compared to men.

On an empirical study conducted in Lucknow, Tiwari S.C. *et al.,* 2012 to study how the older adults are increasing in the country, rapid increasing of nuclear families, the psychosocial problems, and living in a society alone or in an old age home. So, a pilot study was carried out to study the mental health status and morbidities of Old Age Home in Lucknow. The study found that the more of the aging people suffering from mental problems like depression, psychiatric illness, physical morbidity etc.

The study was conducted on the special attention on the aging people and well-being of them by Ming-lin-Chong, A., 2007. The studies conducted the psychological health problems of the elderly and the remedial measures of their problems, role of the professional social workers in individual, family and community level. The study found that the aged were not happy in their life, they were isolated, mentally and physically depressed, unable to talk or share their problems. So, to find out the negative aspects of psychological problems dissatisfaction towards life, unhappy towards their life process and remedial measures of it. The second one is to find out the support systems and network. So, role of social workers to remedies and solve their problems.

From the above review of literature, it is clear that elder people are most vulnerable sections of society. There are several reasons which forced them to take shelter in senior citizen's home. During their old age they became weak both mentally and physically. The most common health problems aged people face include eye sight, hearing, joint pains, nervous disorders, weakness, heart complaints, asthma, tuberculosis, skin diseases, urinary problems, dissatisfactions towards their life, unhappy, mentally depressed, etc. It is observed that most of the studies are conducted in other parts of India. But no known study has been conducted on the lives of elderly people, the reason for shifting their own homes to Senior Citizen's Home of Assam, particularly of the Cachar district of Assam in an institutional setting. Therefore, the present study is an attempt to fill this gap.

The main objectives of the study are:

1. To understand the health problems faced by the elderly in Jeevan Deep Senior Citizen's Home.
2. To study the health consequences of the elderly in Jeevan Deep Senior Citizen's Home.
3. To explore the Health Care Related Services provided by Jeevan Deep Senior Citizen's Home.
4. To study the Problems Faced by Jeevan Deep Senior Citizen's home in delivering the services.

Methodology

The study was conducted in a senior citizen's home, namely, Jeevan Deep Senior Citizen's Home located at Silchar in the Cachar district of Assam. The study is explorative and descriptive in nature. There are 25 respondents out of these, 25 were present during the process of data collection. The data were collected through structured and semi-structured interview schedule with open and close handed questions, focused group discussion, researcher's observation. Further, information related to health care services were collected by interviewing key persons such as superintendent, counsellor, midwives and other staff of the Jeevan Deep Senior Citizen's Home. Direct observation was also made to understand the existing health facilities such as first aid box, oxygen cylinder, sick room etc.

Jeevan Deep Senior Citizen's Home

The Senior Citizen's home was set up in 2004 under the Ministry of Social Justice and Empowerment at Silchar, Cachar, Assam. This Home is established by WOODWICHEE (an NGO); it is a Central Government Scheme, under the Ministry of Social Justice and Empowerment. According to the guideline of the Scheme, there should be 25 inmates in a Senior Citizen's Home. There are nine rooms; each room has four beds, two chairs and a small table and a ceiling fan. There is one office room, one staff room, one kitchen room and one dining room. Besides the home have two bathrooms and four toilets. The home has been set up to provide free food and residential care to the older people. The capacity of the home is twenty five. Presently, fourteen females and ten males are residing in the home. Admission in the senior citizen's home is open to senior men and women who are in the age group of 60 years and above and who have none to support or maintain them. The home provides all the necessary facilities including lodging/boarding, clothing and bedding, counselling services, medical care to all the senior persons. There are six staffs, one male and five female. The staffs include one superintendent, one counsellor, one helper, one midwife, one chowkidar and one cook. During the old age, people become weak both physically and mentally. They are more prone to sickness, diseases, syndromes etc. Few diseases which are common in the old age are diabetes, paralysis, body pain like pain in lower limbs, difficulty in hearing, wrinkling of skin, cannot see properly, shoulder pain, neck pain, back pain, depression and dementia, worsening psychological decline, feeling stress and sense of helplessness etc. Many older persons find living with their adult children to be more difficult than living alone and many do not have a choice and have to live separately from their adult children. In these circumstances, Senior Citizen's home seems to be the choice for the older persons. Though Senior Citizen's homes are a challenge to our culture rich country, it is the need of time as many elderly are rendered homeless and are

Table 15.1: Background details of the respondents

Criteria	Category	Frequency	Percentage
Religion	Muslim	08	32
	Hindu	17	68
Gender	Male	09	36
	Female	16	64
Community	Bengali	25	100
Educational level	Illiterate	13	52
	Primary level	12	48
Age Group (Years)	60-69	14	56
	70-79	08	32
	80 and above	03	12
Marital Status	Unmarried	03	12
	Widow/Widower	22	88
No. of Childrens	No Child	04	14
	Have Childs	21	84
Occupation	Housewife	16	64
	No Work	09	36
Income	No income	25	100

uncared for. It is in this background, the present study is undertaken in a Senior Citizen's home namely, Jeevan Deep Senior Citizen's Home located at Silchar town of Cachar district of Assam to study the health problems of elderly people, the reason for living in this senior citizen's home.

Results and Discussion

Background information: The personal details of the respondents are presented in tabular formation as shown in Table 15.1. The present study observed that majority of the respondents (68%) were from Hindu religion and rest (32%) were from Muslim religion, (36%) of the respondents were male whereas (64%) were female. The majority (52%) of respondents were illiterate and (48%) had up only primary education. It was found that majority (88%) of the respondents were widow/widower and (12%) were married. The majority (56%) of the respondents had age group 60-69 years, (32%) had age group 70-79 years and only (12%) had above 80 years old. By occupation most of the victims (64%) were housewives and rest (36%) were workless. It was also found that (100%) respondents had no incomes.

Health Problems faced by the respondents residing in Jeevan Deep Senior Citizen's Home

Health Problems of the respondents residing in Jeevan Deep Senior Citizens Home: Elderly neglect or abuse can lead to serious consequences, such as bedsores, mentally depressed, gangrene, stroke, broken bones and hematoma. Left unchecked, the neglect of caretakers can result in death. The National Center on Elder Abuse summarizes the many consequences of abuse which seniors experience when they are victimized by nursing homes and caregivers. The impact of abuse is divided into different categories, including: **physical consequences, psychological consequences, financial consequences** and **social consequences. The present study find out the health problem and consequences of the senior citizens' of** Jeevan Deep Senior Citizens Home and the data were presented in Tables 15.2 and Table 15.3.

Table 15.2 reveals that weaknesses, gastric problem, arthritis weakness (25% in each case) are the most common health problems among the senior citizens. Other health problems found among the respondents are body pain, disturbed sleep, mentally depressed, skin problems in 20 per cent, difficulty in hearing 15 per cent, stroke, paralysis in 10 per cent, diabetes per cent and blood pressure are 5 per cent.

Table 15.2: Health Problems of the respondents residing in Jeevan Deep Senior Citizen's Home

Problems	Respondent	Percentage
Blood pressure	1	5
Weakness	5	25
Body pain	4	20
Disturbed sleep	4	20
Gastric problem	5	25
Difficulty in hearing	3	15
Mentally depressed	4	20
Diabetes	1	5
Paralysis	2	10
Arthritis	5	25
Stroke	2	10
Skin problems	4	20

Table 15.3: Distribution of respondents Health Consequences residing in Jeevan Deep Senior Citizen's Home

Health Consequences	No. of Respondent	Percentage
Declining functional abilities	4	16
Increased dependency, sense of helplessness and stress	8	32
Worsening psychological decline	5	20
Depression and dementia	3	12
Malnutrition	5	20

Table 15.3 reveals that (32%) respondents, health consequences are increased dependency, sense of helplessness and stress, (20%) have worsening psychological decline, (20%) have malnutrition, (16%) have declining functional abilities and (12%) have depression and dementia.

Health Care Related Services Provided by Jeevan Deep Senior Citizen's Home

Medical consultation: Doctors visit the senior citizen's home twice in a month on call. They examine the respondents, prescribe medicines and give medicines. However, in case of emergency, the patients are usually sent to Silchar Medical College which is very near to the senior citizen's home.

Health professionals: The Jeevan Deep Senior Citizen's Home is found to be understaffed. There is no permanent position for professional health worker. There is no professional nurse also. However, there is a counsellor in this senior citizen's home. The Midwives is working as a caregiver to the respondents. However, she lacks professional training. The superintendent, counsellor, midwives (caregiver) are responsible for providing medicines, first aid treatment and other medical help as necessary. They also report the patient's complaints and their conditions to the doctor regularly.

Recreational facilities: Recreational activities are very much important for both mental and physical development of the elderly people. Places for entertainment and religious activities are found not available in the Senior Citizen's Home.

Counselling: Regular counselling is provided to the inmates/ respondents as per the needs of the inmates.

Provision of meal according to disease: Food should be provided to the inmates as per their health needs. But such management has been found absent in the senior citizen's home.

Medical record keeping system: The senior citizen's home has medical files of each resident. However, there is no computerized record keeping system.

Problems Faced by Jeevan Deep Senior Citizen's home in delivering their services:

1. **Medical consultation and Health professionals:** In Medical consultation, the Doctors are not attending the patients regularly. There is no permanent position for professional health workers or professional nurse. There is a need to provide regular health care services as per the requirements of the respondents. But the lack of availability of funds the organisation failed to provide such facilities.
2. **Recreational facilities**: Recreational facilities are not enough as it is very much important for both mental and physical development of the elderly people. Places for entertainment and religious activities are found not available in the Senior Citizen's Home.
3. **Counselling:** There is no professional Psychiatrist to provide counselling as per the psychological needs of the respondents.

4. **Provision of meal according to disease**: As per health requirements of the respondents, the nutritious foods are not to be provided. Such management has been found absent in the senior citizen's home.
5. **Medical record keeping system:** There is no computerized record keeping systems, and for that it is difficult to find out correct records and appropriate data related to the respondents as well as organisation.

Conclusion

The study brings out various issues on the lives of elderly people living in Jeevan Deep Senior Citizen's Home. The main focus of the chapter was on health problems and health consequences of the respondents and the major problems faced by Jeevan Deep Senior Citizen's Home. The findings of the study show that female elderly are more in senior citizen's home than male elderly. Majority of the respondents belong to the age group of 60-69, have no source of income. The study reveals that the psychological and physical health problems like changes in mental status (refused to speak, continues speaking), increased dependency, sense of helplessness and stress, malnutrition, worsening psychological decline, declining functional abilities, depression or dementia, weakness, gastric, arthritis are the most common health problems among the respondents. Other health problems found among the respondent are body pain, disturbed sleep, skin disease and mentally depressed for each case, difficulty in hearing and cannot see properly for each, paralysis and stroke for each, blood pressure and diabetes. The home has provided accommodation for elderly people, but there is no enough space for each respondent because of which they are suffering a lot. They are suffering in such a extent which made their life congested within a single room where four respondents are accommodated and all the respondents has to walk a long distance for their daily activities for using latrine, washroom and bathroom. During rainy season there are more chances of injuries. Further, as there is arrangement for four respondent's accommodation in a single room as a result at a single point of time one respondent may be suffering from fever and the other is in need of air which is not possible in such a room. The services provided to elderly are not being able to satisfy the needs of elderly. For example, recreational facilities, routine investigations, food according to specific diseases, computerized health records are the areas which needs to be look into more carefully according to the respondents.

Recommendations

Following recommendations are made to improve the health status of respondents:

1. Recreational facilities should be made available in the senior citizen's homes.
2. For emergency health care facilities like vehicles, doctors etc. should be made available.
3. Health record of the inmates should be computerised.
4. There should be professional health worker and psychiatrist in the senior citizen's home.
5. During the survey it is observed that rooms are not sufficient for respondents. Therefore, more rooms need to be constructed. Single rooms may be best suited for male respondents.
6. There is also a need to introduce income generating activities for the elderly who are fit to work in the senior citizen's homes.
7. A separate sick room should be made available to prevent disease transmission.
8. It is observed in the survey that the respondents have to walk a long distance for their daily activities for using latrine, washroom and bathroom. Therefore, there should be provision for attached latrines and bathroom.

REFERENCES

Balamurugan, J. & Ramathirtham, G., (2012). "Health problem of aged people". *International Journal of Research in Social Sciences*, *2*(3): 140-150. *Constitution of the World Health Organization: Principles*, Retrieved on 7th March, 2018 from http://www.who.int/about/mission/en/

Govil, P. and Gupta, S., (2016). "Domestic Violence against Elderly People: A Case Study of-India". *Advances in Aging Research*, *5:* 110-121. doi.org/10.4236/aar.2016.55011

Iliffe, S., (2016). Community-based interventions for older people with complex needs: time to think again by Oxford University Press on behalf of the British Geriatrics Society, *Age and Ageing; 45:* 2–3. doi: 10.1093/ageing/afv185

Lalon, Y., (2014). "A sociological study of old persons residing in an old age Home of Delhi, India". *International Research Journal of Social Sciences, 3* (4): 21-23.

Ming-lin Chong, A. (2007). "Promoting the Psychosocial Health of the Elderly". *Social Work in Health Care*, *44*:1-2: 91-109. doi.org/10.1300/J010v44n01_08

Nesa, M. A., Haque, Md. E.,. Siddiqua, N.M.R. and Haque, M.I. (2013). "Social status of elderly people in health perspective: A comparison of rural and urban area". *IOSR Journal of Humanities and Social Science, 18* (6): 83-94.

National Policy for Older Persons (1999). Ministry of Social Justice and Empowerment Government of India Shastri Bhawan, New Delhi, http://socialjustice.nic.in/writereaddata/UploadFile/National%20Policy%20for%20Older%20Persons%20Year%201999.pdf

National Policy for Senior Citizens, (2011). Ministry of Social Justice and Empowerment Government of India Shastri Bhawan, New Delhi http://socialjustice.nic.in/writereaddata/UploadFile/dnpsc.pdf

Ramesh, (2013). *Health Status of Elderly Living in the Old Age Homes: An Overview*, pp. 131-141 file:///C:/Users/USER/Desktop/paper/new%20 paper/Health%20Status%20of%20Elderly%20Living_2.pdf

Tiwari, S.C., Pandey, N.M. and Singh, I., (2012). "Mental health problems among inhabitants of old age homes: A preliminary study". *Indian Journal of Psychiatry, 54*(2): 144-148. doi. 10.4103/0019-5545.99533.

Umadevi, L. & Kiran, V.K. (2015). "Issues and challenges of institutionalized old age: Case study report". *The International Journal of Indian Psychology, 2* (4): 36-45.

Index